A WOMAN'S GUIDE TO ADULTERY

BY CAROL CLEWLOW

POSEIDON PRESS
FEBRUARY 1989
NEW YORK   LONDON   TORONTO   SYDNEY   TOKYO

Poseidon Press
Simon & Schuster Building
Rockefeller Center
1230 Avenue of the Americas
New York, New York 10020

Published by the Simon & Schuster Trade Division

POSEIDON PRESS is a registered trademark
of Simon & Schuster Inc.

POSEIDON PRESS colophon is a trademark
of Simon & Schuster Inc.

Designed by Snaphaus Graphics
Manufactured in the United States of America

Lyrics on page 7 © 1979 Pendulum Music Ltd.
Admin. by Warner-Tamerlane Publishing Corp.
All Rights Reserved. Used by Permission.

OR

THINKING OF MONICA

"They do it, they do it, they do it, they do it, again and again,
They do it, they do it, they do it, they do it, married men...."

—Bonnie Tyler, "(The World Is Full of) Married Men"

1

L E T me tell you a joke. It's an old joke. Like all the best jokes. Probably you've heard it before. But never mind. Let me tell you it anyway.

It's about Moses and the Ten Commandments. Moses comes down from the mountain after getting the Ten Commandments from God. At the bottom he sees the Children of Israel waiting. He says, "Look, I've got some good news and some bad news. First the good news. There's only ten. And now the bad news. Adultery's still in."

I like that joke. It's a male joke, the sort of joke told by men in too-tight dinner jackets and too much jewellery, in smokey club rooms to smokey laughter. Still nonetheless, I like it. I like its honesty, its boyishness, its expression of that faint but all-pervading regret which seems to me to accompany the notion of adultery in the male mind. It's a warm joke. Like all good jokes. It makes me laugh. It also makes me want to weep.

Adultery's a good subject for jokes because it's a sad business and the saddest things in life are also, often, the funniest. Life after all is a tragicomedy, a confusion of laughter and tears, of humour and hurt, without so much as a chalk mark to separate the two.

"I never know when you're joking."

"I'm always joking. Only all my jokes are serious."

I said that once to Paul.

And now let me tell you a female joke about adultery. To be frank, it's not really a joke. It's a funny story I like to tell after my fifth glass of wine.

It's about the first married man I went to bed with.

"You won't believe it," I say, "but his name was Romeo. Romeo's a common name in the Philippines."

He made love to me on a dark wood bed, its headboard intricately carved with fruit and flowers, black against the snowy white of the pillows, on a beautiful bed in his hacienda in the soft green Luzon hills.

His love-making was abrupt and unsatisfactory, old-fashioned and devoid of preamble. And yet I almost came from it. Not from the act itself, but from the beauty that surrounded it, from the white linen and the dark bed and from the violet night escaping in through the half-open shutters.

I felt the watery blackness of his hair between my fingers and saw the dark nuggets of his eyes. And so I cried out as he came to his climax, just because of the loveliness of it all, and heard the cry fall back into the air, remote and mysterious and no longer mine.

And then as it fell back on me, I dug my nails into the smooth, shining honey skin of his back, which made him leap away from me, spent as he was, so that we fell apart upon the snowy sheets and pillows.

"Don't scratch my back," he said to me sharply.

• • •

I tell them what he said, my friends, my woman friends. I tell them, "He said, 'Don't scratch my back.'" And we laugh, my woman friends and I, the fine, unfettered laughter of liberated woman at the age-old folly of married man.

He said other things, my Romeo.

He said, "I admire you, Rose," rolling my name out to me between his bright white teeth. "Going off on your own, travelling. You're tough. You can look after yourself. You're not like my wife."

And then he stroked a curious, proprietorial finger around the centre of my left breast. "You have an inverted nipple," he said. "You'll have trouble breast-feeding."

He said that, I remember, the night before he left to return to the capital, to return to his office and his wife and his children.

Yes, he went the next day, leaving me in the care of Luis, who spent each night slumped outside my locked bedroom door, the rifle at his shoulder resting gently between his open knees.

On nights when he allowed himself too much to drink, or perhaps a smoke after dinner, Luis became courtly and chivalrous. He sat guarding me jealously from the farm hands who sang and played music on the verandah, and would not let me dance.

Occasionally when I became angry and rebellious and rose from my seat, I would find him rising, too, beside me, taking my hand and leading me out into the centre of the music, to put his arms stiffly around me, holding me away from his body, to whirl me around to the sound of the accordion and the guitars and to the rhythm of the moths slapping themselves hard and flat against the parchment lampshades as they swooped for the light.

Later, outside the locked door, he would not let himself sleep.

"Everything's all right, Rose," he would mumble, his lips heavy against the keyhole.

"I am here, Rose," he would say softly against the brass.

"Nothing will happen to you, Rose. Not while I'm here, Rose. They must get past me first, Rose."

"Thank you, Luis," I would say in return.

"Goodnight, Rose."

"Goodnight, Luis."

He left Luis at my door and his car at my disposal. But he never called. The days passed into a week and a week into two so that one day I packed my bag and told Luis to take me to the station.

Luis put my bag on the rack above my seat and held out his hand, formally and politely, his eyes opaque and heavy.

I cried all the way back to the capital on the slow, rattling train. The people in the carriage around me tried to comfort me. They brought me strange delicacies, fruits and sweetcakes, laying them in my lap and smiling into my streaming eyes, perplexed and curious.

They spoke to me in American English, direct and un-self-conscious.

"You are very sad," they said gravely. "Crying is no good. You must be happy."

And when I still cried they huddled together in little dark shining groups, staring at me, shaking their heads and chattering in Tagalog.

We laugh, my woman friends and I, over "Don't scratch my back." Sometimes even over the inverted nipple. But not about the tears. I do not tell them, you see, about the tears. I do not tell them about how they came from other parts of the train to watch me weep, how they crammed the doorways and the windows, and sat chattering upon the tops of seats like brightly coloured parrots. Just as I do not tell them about Luis' lips at the keyhole, or his holding me chastely and stiffly, or indeed about his hand pointing politely at my heart in farewell.

I do not tell them because it is not part of the joke, my joke, which may be smart and clever but goes only so far, and being marked out this way, with limits, lacks warmth and is dishonest and hollow and, worse than all of these things, is insufficiently funny.

I do not know why I tell this joke if it does not make me laugh. Perhaps I tell it because it makes me sad. Suffering, I still believe, most often accompanies the notion of adultery in the female mind.

2

M Y friends. My woman friends. We do everything together, my woman friends and I.

We go to the theatre together, to the cinema, to concerts
and exhibitions, to restaurants and rallies and lectures.
Jennifer and Helen at the new Woody Allen film. Rose and
Jennifer try performance art. Rose and Jo and Helen at the
concert for El Salvador.

But tonight we are having dinner at Jennifer's.

I like this best, I think, this dinner at Jennifer's. For
Jennifer's house is beautiful, quite as beautiful as Jennifer,
as pleasing upon the eye, as equally devoid in its appear-

ance of anything harsh or ungentle or generally unsatisfactory.

Yes, Jennifer's house is lovely but suffers from a certain languor, just like Jennifer. For life that is tasteful and tranquil can also be dull. Which is why Jennifer's brass bed drums its fingers beneath the duvet and her cream lace curtains twitch in their sleep.

And why Jennifer's fire licks its lips in the grate, knowing that Jennifer's house like Jennifer waits to be woken with a kiss.

Jennifer will make chilled soup for us, delicate and delicious. Home-made quiche, light as a feather, with one exquisite vegetable, snow peas perhaps, perfectly steamed. She will serve us sorbet and later fine cheeses and fruit and then chocolates, hand-made, small and dark and full of delight.

We shall eat, we women, in a circle, at her large handsome table, its mellow wood pale beneath the light of the lamp.

We shall savour her food and run our fingers over her fine lawn tablecloth. We shall sip from her crystal and stir our spoons in her china and wonder why David does not marry Jennifer.

David should marry Jennifer. David could marry Jennifer. David would marry Jennifer. If it wasn't for Francie.

Francie. All angles where Jennifer is round. All spikey where Jennifer is soft. All lack of grace where Jennifer is lovely. Francie. All bad taste and bitten finger-nail. Black leather and bright blond hair. All polo neck and tiny breasts and thick black lines and stick-thin legs.

David tells Jennifer he's not in love with Francie anymore. He says it's pity now. He says he wants to leave. But Francie gets upset.

David tells Jennifer it's all finished between him and Francie now.

Francie tells Monica things are just difficult at the moment. It's David's work, she says. Driving him mad. But don't worry, she says. It's nothing.

Francie tells Monica they're just going through a bad patch, that's all. And that's what Monica tells Paul and what Paul tells me. It's a highly dependable grape-vine but it breaks down with me. For how can I tell these things to Jennifer?

David says other things to Jennifer. For instance, he says love isn't possession. He speaks it as if the words were in capitals and most often he says it to the cloud of her hair beneath his chin.

He lays his hand flat against the side of her face and with his long slim fingers touches gently the skin around her eyes. He says they must always be honest with each other and he kisses her on the lips, which has the habit of making her head spin with tenderness but also sometimes with confusion so that she lays her head back upon his shoulder to calm herself and also consider how she can feel this cherished and also this cheated.

Jennifer saves the whales and the seals and the natterjack toad and frankly deserves to be happy. She tells me all this with the flames of her fire catching the tumbling brown gold of her hair.

She stares at the fire, over the fruit and the cheese and the coffee cups on the carpet.

"I'm not like you, Rose," she says, turning her eyes, gentle and appealing, from the flames.

"I admire you, Rose," she says, sighing, pulling her full skirt around her knees, lifting her neat little feet from the ground.

"You're not like me, Rose," she says, making a tiny disdainful moue with her pretty lips. "You wouldn't get yourself into this state. Not over a man."

"You're not like any of us, Rose," she says. "You're so sensible, so independent, so..." and she pauses, searching for the word among the flames, the tip of her tongue quivering thoughtfully between her lips, "so self-contained, Rose.

"Really. I don't think you need a man at all.

"But Rose," she says, earnest now and a little breathless with her own bravado, "don't you ever get lonely?"

I told her what I always tell people. That I have friends, many friends, some men, some of them even lovers. Occasionally. Not lately, of course. But as one gets older, it becomes...different, less...easy. I told her all this surprised as always by the defensiveness in my voice, surprised by the shifts in tone from the brisk to the awkward. "And, of course," I told her, "there are my woman friends."

She said "yes" then, hesitantly, doubtfully, and afterwards "yes" again, this time with more certainty, taking a breath, slowly, as if gaining the courage to speak, as if knowing what she was about to say was by way of a confession.

She said, "But it's not the same, is it. I mean they're not the same, are they. However you look at it. Woman friends. However much you like them. However much you love them," she corrected herself, formally, as one speaking a foreign language who makes an error of syntax. "It's not the same, is it. As being with a man, a man that you love."

She looked away again, blushing, to the fire, wistful, a little shameful.

I became as I always become, both prim and placatory, the abbess explaining the ways of the convent.

But she wasn't finished and, as if determined to end what she had begun, broke in on my words.

"Sometimes I'm a little bored when we all go out together," she said, her voice no longer soft but defiant and cool and suddenly very old.

"This gaggle of us. Like a hen party. Women without men. Sometimes I think we're a bit pathetic, really. And I think I'd rather be back here. Back home alone with David."

I think of what she said now, here, with my woman friends, around the table at Jennifer's. I think of what she said with the light from her lamp on our faces. I think of what she said, unmellowed with the wine and tired already of the talk. And I think I should like to be away from here, back home alone. With Paul.

3

Jo generally uses an expletive when talking of Jennifer.

"She's a fucking idiot. Getting herself in a state over that toy-boy. He's almost certainly after her for her money." She raises a friendly but imperious finger at the waiter as if in emphasis.

"He's too old for a toy-boy and you make her sound like an heiress. It's only a small private income."

"Enough to keep him in drugs."

"He smokes a little dope, that's all."

"He's an arrogant, boorish wimp."

"He's not that bad."

"And a lousy poet."

David's poetry is dark and deeply masculine. Staccato lines rattle with obscenities like spent cartridges spitting from a machine-gun. He reads sometimes with rock groups and when he does favours green fatigues.

"They call him post-feminist."

"Which means macho, which makes her a fucking idiot."

It is impossible to sit quietly in the corner with Jo. Her voice is not loud but is well-bred and confident. It rolls out over the tables around us, making the couples, heads bent towards each other, look up quickly and furtively before ducking their heads again in haste lest they be thought shocked or surprised.

They call Jo a man's feminist. By "they" I mean the men with whom she works and sometimes sleeps. And I know what they mean, these men. In the old days, the days to which they still belong, the days before the crystal waters of their socialism clouded with our muddy feminism, Jo would have been a man's woman. Now they accommodate the change by calling her a man's feminist, the new breed of woman, self-taught to demand as a right what the world was so slow to offer.

Jo can pull a waiter to her side quicker than any man I know. She's doing it now, here in this restaurant.

The short, slightly stocky young man has turned his back on two couples who by rights he should have served before us and is bringing his notebook to our table.

He smells trouble from Jo, trouble he wishes to avoid, which is why he turns a deaf ear and a blind eye to the irritated clicks and sighs of the menu-wavers.

He's gay, I imagine, for when did man look that good for woman? He spends time on his tan and on his hair, which falls dark and luxurious over his forehead. He swaggers a little when he walks. He reminds me of Luis.

He knows that if there is trouble she will win and so he turns the pages of his notebook deferentially, half smiling as she patronises him with her searing, unmerciful female courtesy.

He's used to being patronised and accepts it as part of the job. What he cannot accept is the sexuality which surrounds her like a halo, lighting up her bare un-made-up face and her crew-cut fair head.

As he writes he takes a step backwards as if afraid it

will touch him. It disturbs him. Perhaps it distresses him. But in spite of it, or perhaps because of it, he will serve us more attentively than the rest.

I did not argue as I should have done when Jo said what she said about Jennifer. I did not do so because I am a little afraid of Jo. Most people are a little afraid of Jo. Most people, including her lovers.

Often when we are together, we women, I will see her fingers playing with a pen or a fork or the leaves of her programme. I will see smiles flickering in and out of her lips and the lips themselves encouraging the conversation around her. But when I look in her eyes I will see that they are blank and empty as if what she really is has withdrawn to some private space in the back of her head, leaving her body to go on living for the world about her.

"Automatic pilot," I said to her once. "You fly half your life on automatic pilot."

She told me, drunk one night on whisky, that if she found a man more intelligent than herself she would marry him. I think she does not expect to get married. I know she will not marry Martin. She will not marry him even if he leaves Margaret and the children for her, which he would do if she would but ask him. But she will not. For while she likes Martin's tough and battered working-class body and the middle-class love she has taught it to make, and while she even likes his shrewd, sharp self-education, still the game they play, in bed and out of it, pretending to be equal, is exactly that. Just a game.

Martin, when very drunk, which is not uncommon now, will say that he owes everything to Jo. He will say, "How could she do it?" throwing the question out like a drowning man hurling a life-belt to himself.

"She put me there," he will say, slurring his words, full of pride, bravado and shame. "They wanted her. The party members wanted her. She should have had it. But a woman like her? In a union seat?"

And then he will draw me in closer as we stand side by side at the bar. He will put an arm around my shoulder, his other hand clutched around his drink.

"She lost out and then she threw herself behind me," he

will say. "She got me in instead. How could she do that?"

And then he will shake his head and raise his eyes while all the time she clicks her tongue and grimaces, saying, "For God's sake, Martin . . ." or, "Don't be ridiculous, Martin" or, "Shut up, Martin" or some other short sharp phrase of irritated disregard.

It's four years now since Martin was elected, four years in which his children have grown older, his wife cooler and more distant.

The affair has trundled quietly on, kept from the light by the shadows of Jo's other lovers and the dark figure too of Margaret, who despite everything still appears at her husband's side, the good constituency wife, at the fêtes and the fun runs and the school speech days.

Poor Margaret?

I do not know. I only know she looks less attractive than she did when I first met her four years ago. She looks tired now, pinched, not thinner, for indeed she has put on some weight, around the waist and the thighs, where women do put on weight when middle age appears on the horizon and they ponder seriously, for the first time, the opposing virtues of sexual attraction and good, satisfying food.

Poor Margaret?

I do not know. I only know that the perm that turned her head overnight into a mass of curls straggles untidily now around her shoulders, a sign to those who know about such things that either Margaret cannot afford a new one or is in such a state of peculiarly female despair that she doesn't give a damn about the state of her hair.

Poor Margaret?

I do not know. I only know what Jo says, which is "God knows why she stays with him," dragging out the "knows" at the same time pulling a cigarette from a packet to light it with a sharp dismissive flick of her fingers.

"She loves him," I want to say but never do, being especially nervous of her when she is sharp and dismissive like this.

And why should she love him? Why should she love him after four years of disintegrating married life? Four years tailed by her husband's adultery. Four years hearing its foot-fall, catching it out of the corner of her eye. Four years of the soft, sickening realisation sneaking up on her and sitting on her shoulder and finally whispering in her ear that her husband is sleeping with somebody else.

Why should she love him? Why after all should she not have stayed with him because of the children, or the house or the car, because of finances or appearances, or simply because it was more convenient that way?

Why, in fact, should she not prefer it? Why should she not rather be without Martin's attentions? Why should she, a Catholic with three children at her skirts, not be happy to be done with all his love-making, not knowing that under Jo it has become so much more subtle and luxurious, so much more in tune with the infinitely delicate descant of female desire than when he lay on her before and gave her first their daughter and then their two fine sons?

Why should she not prefer it?

She should not prefer it because of me. Because *I* prefer she loves him. Because *I* want her to care. Because *I* want her to be unhappy and to suffer.

Because this is the way I think wronged wives ought to behave, the way in which they should act to best express the utter misery of their plight, the nature of their wrong.

You see, the truth is that privately I disapprove of adultery.

4

YES, the truth is that I disapprove of adultery, or at least, I disapprove of Jo's kind of adultery, cold, unconcerned, dismissive. I think if there has to be adultery, it should be full of angst, full of proper visible pain. Like Helen's.

Here, look. The company notepaper. Three names slanting lazily along the bottom where once they stood to attention to accommodate a fourth. Michael. Helen's husband.

They joked and joshed with Michael in the basement where the pressmen and the PRs meet to drink their gin and tonics and make passes at the secretaries. They gave

him a tankard suitably inscribed and, in voices over-loud
with drink and shallow bonhomie, called him "the opposition" and shouted, "Watch out, Ray," across the bar so that
Michael had to mumble pompously about "pastures new"
and "time for change," knowing nobody was fooled.

Which left the three names, Ray's and Helen's and Sandra's. Sandra. Wife of Ray. Sandra, who has not set foot
among the grey and black and silver chrome since the day
she came to tell him she was pregnant. Sandra, who, walking unannounced into his office, found him and Helen
standing very close together and divined by the way they
parted, sharply, turning their heads away, reaching blindly
and without purpose for paper, pens and folders, that they
had been embracing.

In the old days Michael might have had to fight a duel.
Kill or be killed. Still he must do the honourable thing. At
forty, in a shifting quicksand of a business, he must sacrifice the security of Ray's payroll. He must squeeze himself
out between the names and slide off the bottom of the page.
He must walk off with a wave into the mediocre sunset
that awaits the unambitious, the moderately talented and
those approaching middle age.
And, too, he must leave the rather too expensive, rather
too large executive home for a chill compact little flat. He
must leave the fridge and the washing machine in exchange for the stereo.
And of course he must leave Andy.

Michael knew that Helen and Ray were having an affair.
It hurt at first. But he endured the pain, numbing it, as
was perfectly convenient, with drink. And then he found to
his surprise that he could live with it. Given help and encouragement he could even forget it. Yes, he could forget
all about the affair when he took Andy fishing or to the
football or just to do the late night shopping when Helen
was still at work.
For searching around in the pain of losing Helen's love,
searching for what meant the most to him in life, he found
he loved Andy with a passion, loved him even more for the
accidental way in which he had seemed to arrive.

They had tried early on in the first romantic flush to have a child but had failed, and soon their life grew into a certain pattern. It was a pleasing pattern, a pattern that suited them both separately and together, and they didn't say, although they thought, it was a pattern that could only be changed by a child.

When Helen became pregnant, seven years after they had married, they had to forage around in their minds to find the time that they had made love. The memory, when discovered, proved to be awkward and embarrassing to both of them, a limp, unsatisfactory coupling one Sunday tea-time after a long expansive lunch at Ray and Sandra's.

Yes, he could forget all about Helen and Ray when he was with Andy. But something in Helen could not let him.

Cast up together on an absurdly inappropriate romantic weekend away laid on by a client, Helen insisted on telling him about the affair, forced it upon him in a row which exploded out of nowhere the moment they entered the chintzy, oak-beamed bedroom.

She lay upon the four-poster, propped up upon the pillows, sipping the champagne delivered to their room and playing with a long-stemmed rose she had pulled from a vase by the bed.

She stared into the air as she talked, seeming not to care as she spoke that she blasted away the ground from beneath his feet, that she took the life that he had made in her hands and crumpled it up and threw it aside like so much litter.

She turned the rose in her fingers and told him she was sorry. She said they had tried so hard not to have an affair. She said it with eyes earnest and full of the need to be believed. She said they had always been close. Caring so much about the business as they did. They had known they were attracted. They tried not to give in.

"But you know how it happens," she said.

She recited the circumstances of their adultery in a dull, flat voice as though starving them of any show of emotion would make their recitation the less embarrassing, the less distressing. She even named the account they were working on. She pronounced it with an appeal in her voice as though the name might make the offence the more explicable, perhaps even the more pardonable.

She tried to draw him into her conspiracy. They had been away. They had had too much to drink. How foolish. How forgiveable.

"You know how it is," she said.

They had tried to stop it. Of course they had tried to stop it. For his sake. For Sandra's. And, of course, for the children's. But they had been unable to do so. It had been too strong. Too important. Too special.

She was drunk by this time from the champagne. She made the mistake of trying to tell him what it meant to her. What it had felt like that first time. She fumbled among the clichés and the clumsy phrases. She said it had been like coming home, like something for which she had waited for a long time. She said it was different. And then, as if realising her folly, she drained off the end of the champagne and, lowering the bottle to the bedside table, became brusque. She said she was sorry. But she needed Ray. And she believed they needed each other.

"I need you," said Michael then, speaking for the first time, a last gulp of champagne making his brain fizz and the tears start behind his eyes. "I need you and Andy needs you and Andy needs us both," he finished slyly.

She looked up at him then, her eyes hard and suspicious and angry. She knew what he was going to say. She knew he had compromise in his heart and she turned away not wanting to hear it.

And so they went down to dinner because upset as they were they were also hungry after their journey.

At the dinner table Michael was adult and kind. Perhaps it was his finest hour, his best ever public relations exercise.

Pulling from a secret pocket the hidden card of his seven years' extra wisdom and experience, he became, suddenly, no longer the husband, instead an old friend, someone without side, without an axe to grind, someone who could be trusted.

He chose the wine, solicitously suggested the vegetables, shook out her napkin as if she was just a little young, or just a little sick.

He pretended, as she became drunker, to play devil's advocate. He pretended to play it purely in the pursuit of truth, in the search for a solution which would suit them both, which would enable the two of them to be hurt as little as possible.

"Damage limitation," he said with a friendly smile, raising his glass to her in a chaste, asexual toast.

When he saw that she was very drunk, he let her have it straight between the eyes.

He said Ray would never leave the boys. He said yes, frankly, he was sure that she was right if she thought Ray was bored with Sandra. Of course Ray was bored with Sandra. Any intelligent man would be bored by Sandra. But Sandra had the boys. And therefore she had Ray.

Ray, he said again, lightly almost, turning away, dropping the spoon to the crème caramel as if this only were important, Ray, he said, would never leave the boys.

She tried to fight back but she was like a child throwing snowballs against a steel door, which stick with a slap as they strike it and begin, almost immediately, to disintegrate, becoming slushy and wet and sliding finally down in a thin stream of cold grey water.

She tried. She repeated things she had said before like "I love Ray" and "Ray loves me" as if they were spells or charms. But in the end the flatness in his voice defeated her, the flatness which was somehow so much worse than the flatness, earlier, in hers.

For hers had been a defiant flatness. She had said such things as "Ray loves me and I love Ray" flatly and without emotion in the very hope that saying them this way, forthrightly, as if merely stating the case, might somehow catapult events forward, might collapse them and re-form them in the shape in which she wanted them to be.

But his flatness had an air of finality about it. The words came out deep and full and amplified with confidence. They rendered her helpless. Worse than that, they reminded her of something she did not wish to remember. They reminded her she had no real evidence to lay before him that he was wrong.

They reminded her that Ray had never yet said he was going to leave Sandra.

And so Michael persuaded her to try again.

After dinner she climbed the wide handsome staircase ahead of him like a bad-tempered child sent to bed early, dragging her feet and dragging also a recalcitrant hand upon the bannister.

In bed he tried to seal their understanding with an innocent kiss, the kiss of a friend, but she misinterpreted his action and turned away from him abruptly, withdrawing to the other side of the massive oak bed.

It lasted six months, the trying again. The atmosphere in the house grew colder and darker with each day. Shadows appeared beneath Helen's eyes like smuts from the smog of misery around her. She breathed heavily when Michael was around her, snapped at him when he spoke to her, but what was worse, went then to the bedroom and closed the door and wept, hour after hour refusing to speak to him.

One night when they were alone and Andy was with his grandparents, she screamed into his face, "I'm having an affair. Don't you understand, I love him. I love him. Why don't you go?"

She was drunk, lying upon the expensive, over-stuffed leather sofa, the whisky bottle and the soda siphon beside her on the carpet. She was in her dressing gown although it was still early in the evening. Her make-up was slipping down her face with her tears. She looked old.

He looked at her and saw himself too and felt sorry for the pair of them.

That night he moved into the spare bedroom, and the next day, sitting quietly together on the sofa, they told Andy.

The boy sat between them, his hands in theirs, as they told him Daddy was leaving. He looked more puzzled than upset. He furrowed his brow and said, "Why? Don't you love Mummy anymore?" They were astonished that a question could be so impossible. And they were lost and quite unable to answer.

He put his arms around Andy and wept into his fair hair, and when he felt his head growing wet too, realised Helen was doing the same to him. They stayed that way together, the three of them, for a long while, locked together like three figures in a sculpture of soft, unfired clay.

• • •

He had been quite sure, you see, that he spoke the truth when he told Helen that Ray would never leave Sandra.

Often Ray joined Andy and himself at the football with Benjamin and Mark, and watching him he had seen his own tender wondering passion for his son mirrored in the other man's eyes.

He reasoned, understandably, that he was a father and only he could know what the boys meant to Ray.

And then, by chance, he found out what Ray meant to Sandra.

He phoned her, one night, drunk and bitter in his unwarmed, unwelcoming flat. He looked around at the bare walls and the too-few sticks of furniture and, all of a sudden, he wanted someone to be unkind to. And, all of a sudden, it seemed logical that the someone should be Sandra.

Her voice when she answered the phone was neutral and cool but turned wary and unhappy when she realised it was him. He could tell immediately that she knew why he was phoning, that she knew what he had to say and did not want to hear it.

Where was Ray? he asked. He was away, she said. Overnight. At a meeting.

"With Helen?" asked Michael, his voice rising sharply with derision and also with the drink.

There was silence then at Sandra's end of the phone, a silence into which Michael began to pour all his bitterness. He tried to flay her with his own unhappiness. He tried to burn her. He closed his eyes, imagining with pleasure the scorch marks and the bruises upon her face.

He told her times and places. As a joke he even told her the names of the clients, as Helen had done. "While you were sitting at home, Sandra," he said. "Why don't you and I go out now, Sandra, and enjoy ourselves?"

Afterwards he had been so ashamed of himself, so very ashamed. She had put the phone down with a click in the middle of his torrent of words, and he had hung his head and cried, still holding on to the receiver, using it to brush away a drunken tear.

He had tried to phone her back to say he was sorry, but there was no answer, and he knew that she had unplugged the phone, which made him weep a little more.

And yet nothing happened.

Helen never spoke of it and neither did Ray when he and Andy bumped into him with the boys at the football. Which meant Sandra had told no one, which is when he became even more certain that Ray would not leave Sandra.

He saw then that Sandra had told no one because she believed she could ride out the storm. He saw that she wanted, more than anything, to hold on to Ray, and she thought if she stayed silent, kept her head, went quietly on, she could do so. And he, Michael, believed she was right.

Michael told me what he had done one lunchtime when I saw him, unexpectedly, in a bar near the university.

"Help the unemployed, Rose," he said. "Buy the jobless a drink."

He was drunk and demanding, pulling me away from the people I was with, his grip tight upon my arm.

Later at a table in the corner he said, "It's no good, Rose. I can't make it on my own. I'm not cut out for it. I'm not a businessman. I'm a hack. You understand that. We're both hacks, you and I. That's how we started. That's what we are. We should never have got into the PR business. Either of us.

"I'm going back into newspapers, Rose," he said, staring at his cigarette as he tapped it with deliberation in the ashtray.

"I've been doing the rounds trying to get a job. Buying drinks for people who were kids when I started. Editors now. Chief reporters.

"It's made me realise that I'm old, Rose," he said.

"I'm old, Rose," he repeated, his eyes fastened still to his cigarette. "I'm old and I'm frightened."

"No, Michael," I said, "you're drunk and there's a difference. You'll get a job. It just takes time, that's all."

He told me everything then, about the parting, about the phone call. He became by turns maudlin, ashamed and defiant.

"I'll bet Helen never told you anything about it," he said, lifting his pint glass to his lips.

"No. She just told me you'd split up, that's all."

"That's Helen all over," he said, leaning towards me, leering a little. "Private...secretive. She never tells anyone about herself. Not even her friends. Sometimes I think she's a little crazy."

"Nonsense."

"No really, it's not natural." He shook his head as he spoke, his face crumpling suddenly in drunken self-complacency. "She won't tell you anything. Even when she's hurting. Even when she's in pain."

He lowered the glass to the table, scorn darkening the self-complacency like a cloud.

"She just goes on," he said, "suffering in silence."

I put some money down on the table for the food, but he grabbed my hand as I rose to go, scattering the coins upon the floor.

"He won't leave the boys, you know," he said urgently, half rising from his seat. "I've told her but she won't believe me. Perhaps she'll believe you."

"I doubt it," I said, pulling my hand out of his.

He drew back then, his eyes still fixed upon mine, the look of scorn re-settling upon his face.

"She'll go on year after year," he said, "waiting for him. What a fool."

He raised the empty glass once more at me as if in a toast, at the same time raising little boy's eyes, brimming with the need to be wicked.

"Women," he said. "They're so stupid. So bloody stupid. Really, they must like to suffer."

5

Is it true then, what Michael said?

Is he right? Do we like to suffer, we women?

Do we pick our lovers deliberately unfree and encumbered to cause us some pain so pure and delicate and satisfying that it is also pleasure, a pain caused by the heartstrings beginning to quiver with love, beginning to tighten and at last, slowly, beginning to tear?

Is it true then?

I am not just unhappy sitting at this table, crumbling my roll opposite Jo. I am surprised at my own unhappiness and it is this surprise, that it should have happened this way, which gives the extra cutting edge to my unhappiness.

I stand behind myself at the table, a ghostly attendant, leaning wickedly and deferentially towards myself, speaking Jennifer's words in my ear in a mocking, gleeful whisper.

"You're not like them, Rose," I say. "You wouldn't get yourself in such a state. Not over a man."

The words jangle in my head. They leap up and down in a frenzied dance. They lunge and stab at the fabric of my self-possession.

If I had the courage to say to Paul the simple words "You are destroying my peace of mind," this is what I should be trying to say. I should be trying to say "You are destroying not just what I am but what I remember myself to be, what the 'I am' was built on.

"You are destroying even what I was."

I sat outside his study in my one good suit with my one good exam result in my brief-case beside me. I was early. Probably female mature students always are. On the other side of the door his phone rang continually with a hopeful, insistent ring.

He arrived twenty minutes late, the picture of the absent-minded professor, arms spilling with books, shedding paper as he turned the key to let us into his room, his apologies dissolving gracefully in the warmth of his greeting.

"I'm so sorry...Rose, isn't it...we've met I think... you're a friend of..."

"...Jo's...yes...at one of her parties I think...you were there with..."

"Monica...yes...with my wife Monica."

I was irritated by him, his lateness, his overt, unashamed charm. But even more I was annoyed at myself, at my sense of something sensible and scornful slipping away in the face of that charm and in the face of his archetypal academic good looks and curious air of languorous enthusiasm.

Inside, though, my irritation all but disappeared, for I was charmed by his room, charmed, of course, as only a thirty-five-year-old woman hungry to read English can be charmed.

Books rose to the ceiling, as I had always imagined they should. A threadbare imitation Persian rug stretched upon the parquet at the feet of a battered sofa half-hidden with mountains of files and books and papers. Beneath the window a radiator hissed very gently, while outside a tree waved a friendly branch against the glass.

He made me coffee, talking in a relaxed and humorous way about himself, about the minor crisis which had made him late. He had taken his wife to the dentist. An emergency. Such pain. Wisdom teeth apparently. Developed in her thirties. Good Lord. How unusual.

I closed my eyes listening to his voice as he spooned the coffee into the cups, his back towards me.

Of all the things about him, I think now it was his voice I loved the most.

It was light and easy and many-layered, as if packed full of all the good things in life which made him what he was, his public school, his Cambridge first, his famous family. It was precise and pleasant with undistorted vowels, warm and unassumingly friendly. But overlaying all this was a coolness, a dismissiveness, which in others might have been offensive, giving an impression of superiority, but in him was somehow self-effacing, as if he was trying to tell you that actually all that he was faintly embarrassed him, and in the absence of anything else he thought it best to apologise for it.

It was as I sat there, letting the loveliness of his voice wash over me, that he rounded on me suddenly, thrusting the mug of coffee in my hand.

Why did I want to read English? What books did I read? Why did I like them? What did I know?

I found I knew nothing. A few stock names edged out nervously between my lips along with incoherent, half-understood phrases about them. These he shot down as soon as they were spoken, reaching at the same time leisurely for a packet of French cigarettes lying by his elbow upon the desk.

Watching him light the cigarette I felt the last reserves of confidence drain away. I felt my face flushing with embarrassment at my own ignorance. I became flustered. I stuttered and stumbled. I spilt my coffee. And then the phone rang and he reached across the desk to answer it, turning away from me and putting me out of my misery.

It rang almost continuously after that, as if by divine intervention, each time he fired at me another of his impossible questions.

I took advantage of it, pausing as his question struck me, looking into space as if choosing my words, furrowing my brow, opening my mouth, spinning out the last few seconds until the phone rang again, till I could look regretfully at the instrument and ruefully but admiringly at him as he picked it up, raising his eyebrows at me and grimacing, no longer my interrogator but my associate, sharing with me a sympathetic understanding of the ceaseless irritations and responsibilities of the adult working life.

Later when we came to know each other better we laughed about that interview.

He was surprised to discover that I had answered so few of his questions. He remembered me as thoughtful... interesting... promising.

Faced with a hopelessly incomplete image of me, he had sketched in the gaps for himself, shaded me in, made me whole again. And why not? Don't we all do it?

Later on I did the same for him and came to all the same conclusions. Thoughtful... interesting... promising.

When I started my degree the following autumn, I found out why his phone had rung so continuously.

He dominated the department.

Those who knew no better took him for its head rather than his elderly retiring superior, who hid behind his secretary in a small suite of rooms, emerging once a year to lecture on Milton, his eyes fixed firmly over his students' heads as if the sight of them distressed him.

Paul ran the literary society and the literary magazine. He directed occasional productions for the university drama group. He arranged field trips to Brontë country and to Wordsworth's cottage. He put together intriguing seminars, with wine, on television soap operas and thrillers and romantic best-sellers.

He sat on the committee which organised the town's literary festival and liaised with the local arts council. He gave lectures in the evening at the adult education centre and in the odd spare hour in the afternoon shot across town to the outlying estates to run writing classes for women and for the young unemployed.

"Sometimes I think this is the stuff that really counts, Rose," he would say wistfully, earnestly, leaning towards me, his eyes bright with the extravagant enthusiasm with which he teased from the unacademic their halting inarticulate ideas.

"You can get away with so much more with a roomful of students than you can with these people," he would say, leaning back, blowing lazy meditative smoke rings in the air.

Meanwhile his university students passed through his study in a continual stream.

They came with their problems, with their hopes and their fears, with their failures and their successes.

They came to him shaking with rage after arguments with other lecturers, shaking with nerves before exams, shaking with tears after broken love affairs.

He bucked them up and calmed them down. He rapped their knuckles and wiped away their tears. He made phone calls for them and wrote letters, to their parents, to their prospective employers, to their doctors, even sometimes to their bank managers.

He took them for a drink when they needed encouragement, to pizzerias and Indian restaurants when they were miserable. He gave them lifts home from parties when they were drunk and took them to the sanatorium when they were sick.

In return they sent letters which layered upon his notice-board. "Just to say thank-you"... "Without you I can't imagine"... "I simply don't know what I would have done."

"It's hard these days being young, Rose," he would say. "Of course we had it so much easier in the sixties."

Wherever we saw him he was enthusiastic and boyish and joyful, circulating easily among the students, re-filling their glasses, drawing the shy ones from the corners into the cliques of the confident and self-assured.

And then one day we glimpsed a different Paul.

• • •

It was in the second year. When he gave his lecture on Conrad. His speciality.

It was spring, and the bright early March sun shone mercilessly in through the high, arched windows of the lecture theatre.

He arrived ten minutes late for the early morning lecture, his skin chalky and his eyes bloodshot.

His pleasant, handsome face, usually so open and smiling, was closed and grim and unfriendly. He dropped his books upon the table at the front of the room with a thud which rose up both defiant and defeated.

He began immediately to speak without opening a book as if of the opinion that the task to be the more quickly completed must be the sooner begun.

He spoke the words without conviction or enthusiasm, as though they were old thoughts which he now knew too well and of which he had grown tired. And as he spoke his strained, fiery eyes roved over my head and over the heads of the other mature women students congregated in the front row, faces lifted towards him, embarrassingly near and embarrassingly naked with the ravenous desire for knowledge.

I felt sorry for him, all of a sudden, confronted with such hunger, weak and ill as he was, and as if detecting my sympathy his eyes dropped and caught mine.

For a moment they held and I saw in them an appeal for pity. I saw desperation and unhappiness and sheer tiredness fighting for space. But what surprised me was what came after, in the last fraction of a second, before he looked away.

For in his eyes then I saw dislike, chilly, resentful and unmistakable.

In the third year he became my tutor. My tutor. And Jennifer's. Of course. Who else but Jennifer? Jennifer sitting upon the imitation Persian rug, stretching out her adorable pointed toes, bringing exquisite home-baked biscuits neatly packed in a little plastic box.

Soon after we began our tutorials, Paul abandoned his cheap instant coffee and bought an Italian coffee pot. Jennifer went to the market then and bought mis-matching bone china cups. Later on he started bringing in the occasional bottle of wine, and so Jennifer went to the market again and came back with cheap cut glass goblets.

The tutorials started at three and were supposed to last for an hour. Often we were still there at five. Sometimes we adjourned to a pub, occasionally even to a restaurant.

Jennifer sat upon the rug in front of the radiator, and I stretched out behind her on the sofa. Paul sat in his black canvas director's chair and the phone sat silent and unplugged, the ultimate compliment, upon the desk.

There was a thin, delicate sensuality in the air, arising not from ourselves but from the words that we spoke and agreed upon and argued over, a sensuality whipped up by the gentle melancholy perception of days numbered that belongs to the older student.

We talked and we laughed and sometimes we even quarrelled. Once Jennifer wept and had to be comforted when she and I disagreed violently over D. H. Lawrence.

Jennifer loved Lawrence. Things said against him hurt her in some oddly personal way. She would lift her eyes to me when I spoke against him and say, "But Rose, Lawrence is why I am here. Lawrence is why I came to university," as if this was the last word on the subject, as if because of it nothing more could be said. And, indeed, more often than not, it was not.

But this time I was full of wine and could not be stopped, even by Jennifer's eyes, soft with the suggestion of tears.

For Jennifer sitting hurt and unhappy upon the rug made me angry and so did Paul, stretching back in his seat, as if politely withdrawing from an argument in which his interest was limited, concentrating instead upon blowing perfect patronising smoke rings.

"How can you like him so much, Jennifer?" I demanded of her. "Tell me what you see in him."

"His prose is so wonderful," she said, staring up and out at the sky, her voice breathy with adoration.

"Oh yes, wonderful prose. We all know his prose is wonderful. But what he says with it is so thoroughly unpleasant."

"To you, Rose. To you," said Jennifer, looking down now

and quietly scraping a lovely half-mooned finger-nail across the rug.

"To me, Jennifer? To any normal woman, Jennifer, the man hates women. I use the word advisedly. He's offensive. He goes against everything we are. Don't you see that? The phallus as the only source of pleasure, anal sex as the ultimate good time and masturbation a hanging offence."

I saw her stir and open her mouth to speak, and so I rushed on.

"And despite all this still the man won't go away. Still he seems to have some place in the British public conscious-ness as the arbiter of sexual liberation, the high priest of love. Goddamn it, his sexual preferences are *still* dictating the way sex is written about in this country, still spawning the sort of erroneous crap that men write about women."

"Oh come now," said Paul, leaning forward sharply as if scenting that the heart of the matter was being ap-proached. "Come now. Surely you're not saying that no man has written well about women. Some men surely have written very well about women?"

"Oh really. Who? And how would you know? How the fuck would you know what it's like to be a woman?"

The obscenity was violent and ugly and out of place, vi-brating in the air long after it had been spoken. After it there was silence. We looked away from each other and down into our wine glasses. In the quiet my anger began to melt away. I looked up to find Paul staring at me, his face concerned and embarrassed. He looked as though he was afraid I had gone too far, for my own safety and for my own peace of mind.

"You are so ... presumptuous," I said to him, shaking my head, both irritated and excited by his concern.

But then I smiled, conscious of liking him very much. I touched Jennifer's head with my hand, a foolish apologetic little pat, and she leaned her head back at me, her short ponytail dancing in forgiveness.

"I understand what you're saying, Rose," she said. "I know he doesn't fit in with the times now, sexually. But what he wrote was written in sincerity, Rose. A man trying sincerely to make sense of sex, in his own way, idio-syncratic as it may appear to us now. And of course it seems old-fashioned today. But what's new today will be old-fashioned one day. Your novel could be old-fashioned one day, Rose."

Paul leapt up joyfully from his seat then, with the bottle in his hand, and began re-filling Jennifer's glass.

"Rose," he said, "how splendid. I didn't realise you'd written a novel."

"Writing. Still writing. I'm going to submit it for my finals."

"Splendid," he said again. "No men in it, I presume," he added, roguishly. "If men can't write about women, clearly the reverse applies."

"Clearly," I said, looking at him, overcome all of a sudden with sadness. "Yes, there are men. But I expect you to treat them as I treat Miriam or Ursula or Constance Chatterley. With the gravest suspicion. The problem with creating male characters is that you only have your own feelings to go on, not the feelings of men themselves. You don't know how they think. Only how you think they should think."

"Maybe that goes for all characters, Rose," said Jennifer quietly, lifting her head again to me. "Maybe it's not just the men.

"Maybe that goes for your women as well."

It was the week after that the snow fell.

Something wonderful happens during an unexpected snow fall. A delicious sense of emergency appears out of nowhere. Standards fall without warning. Time-tables lapse. There's a feeling abroad that things may be allowed normally considered quite out of the question.

Jennifer phoned to say the car wouldn't start and she would be late. Paul looked at the sky and told her not to bother. And so it was just the two of us.

Well, the two of us and Lawrence. He wouldn't go away. He hung around from the previous week, a malevolent voyeur, old-fashioned perhaps, but curiously enduring in the face of such all-pervading female scorn.

"It simply isn't possible for a feminist to accept him. We're talking about masculine supremacy here. The cult of the masculine. The fact is that things like the Hite report show that sexually it isn't the way Lawrence thought it was, the way he wanted to pretend it could be. We don't want what he wanted us to want. We women need Lawrence like a hole in the head, Paul. You simply can't go on teaching him like feminism had never happened."

"Yes, I think you have a point. But what worries me is I think you're really rather blinkered over Lawrence. You see what you want to see. There's a tenderness there that you're totally ignoring."

"Ignoring? No. I just can't see it. All I see is supremacy. The seat of female satisfaction lodged firmly and unequivocally in the male. The female forever an underling in a sexually fascist male regime."

"No. I have to disagree. It's not just about supremacy, for one side or the other. There's a yearning there for a conjunction of male and female, for a merging of the soul. You must see it."

"A yearning? How can you think that? The opposite. A horror of it. Surely you can see that. He cannot desire a twinning of the souls because for him it can only end up with man being completely overpowered and emasculated by the suffocating femaleness of woman. Herein surely lies the neurotic fear he has for the fate of poor old John Thomas faced with Lady Jane. He sees her gaping like a praying mantis waiting to swallow him up. I think he felt that there was a fundamental truth of sexual relations which only he was permitted to see, that love is the female revenge. That love allows the female to swallow up the male and spit him out again as male children branded forever with the mark of the female beast."

How can you stop when you are talking this way? At tea-time? On a Thursday?

How can you not continue over a drink, making the offer casually, apologetically, making it sound of no consequence. Blaming the snow.

"Well, there's no point in going to my night class."
"No one will turn out on a night like this."

And how can you fight the feeling of well-being that rises within you with a drink in your hand and an attrac-

tive, interesting man on the other side of the table?
"I'm hungry. Are you?"

And what do you, the pair of you, do after your second
glass of wine at your favourite Italian restaurant, when
you're beginning to feel warm and close and in some odd
way insidiously special to each other?
You begin to talk about yourselves, that's what you do.
Both of you. You grab the opportunity with open arms, a
small untruthful voice at the back of your head telling
you never mind, you can stop when you like and not to
worry because everyone needs nights like these and afterwards you can always laugh it off or blame the wine.
Or the snow.

"Of course I love what I do. I mean the teaching really is
everything to me, particularly the outside stuff. But I've
come lately to feel I need something else as well. Actually
I've been approached to do an Open University programme
on Conrad. I've had an audition. They liked my voice, ap-
parently."
"Oh, you do have a wonderful voice."
"Now you're mocking."
"No. Really. It's one of the first things I noticed about
you."
"What about you? After the exams."
"Back to work, I suppose."
"What about writing?"
"Well yes, but I mean I've only written this one thing so
far and I don't know if it's any good."
"If you'd like me to read it for you, of course I'd be de-
lighted."
"Oh really. Well, yes, as a matter of fact that would be
very helpful. I'd love you to read it. Although of course it
will be terrible. Having someone actually look at it I
mean."
"'There's something tragic and displeasing about a
woman who writes.'"
"Don't tell me. Lawrence."
"Who else? So what about the novel then? Male characters that I have to distrust. Right?"

"And female characters, too, according to Jennifer."

"And no lusty sex scenes? None of that old John Thomas and Lady Jane stuff, I trust?"

"Certainly not."

"Why aren't you married, Rose?"

"I don't need a husband."

"No?"

"No. What I need is a wife. A wife to keep the flat clean and cook for me. A wife to stay in and wait for the repair man when the washing machine breaks down. A wife to take the car to the garage for repair, to remember to buy cat food and toilet rolls. Actually I've asked several of my girl friends to marry me, but for some reason they've all refused. I think they think we're too much alike."

We were still laughing when I said, right in the middle of it, "And what about Monica?"

And when I had said the words I was surprised that they had been said, so that when I heard them dying away in the air, I could scarcely believe that they were mine.

They brought the conversation sharply to a halt, as if we had been cantering, the two of us, in harness, pulling it along between us, side by side, hooves flying, nostrils flaring, and as if some voice not ours cried, "Whooa there," drawing us to a halt, so that now we stood, snorting and stamping and chafing at the bit.

"Ah Monica," he said. "Yes, Monica."

He stared hard at a spoonful of profiteroles as he raised it to his lips, as if the words he needed might be hidden there among the moons of pastry, chocolate and cream.

"I cannot say," he said, "I am unhappy with Monica, for Monica does not make me unhappy. I cannot say I cannot live with Monica, for Monica is perfectly easy to live with. I cannot say with the travelling salesman that my wife does not understand me, for I suspect she understands me very well. I cannot even say I do not love my wife.

"But..." he said, "but..." turning his eyes to my face as if now quite sure the words were written there.

"But something's gone?"

"Yes."

"You're no longer *in love* with Monica."

• • •

And there it lay on the table between us, our first cliché, hiding between the black pepper and the rock salt, nestling the Parmesan cheese, staring up at us, a couple at a table in the corner, intellectualising and idealising and seeking reasons why they cannot be just like all the other couples at tables in corners in restaurants around the world who are about to embark like them on that most predictable, most unadventurous, most singularly unoriginal of pastimes, the extra-marital affair.

Perhaps it brought us to our senses, that cliché. Perhaps it woke us up, for we surfaced not long afterwards from the wine and from the conversation and, looking around the restaurant, found it to be empty except for the waiters who crowded around a table in the corner talking heatedly with wide exuberant gestures.

They waved aside our apologies. They brought the bill and accepted a large tip with charm, waving us off like lovers, blessing us somehow with their warmth and their gallantry, making what happened later not just right and proper but perfectly inevitable.

Later, at home, he said, "I must go," but still did not move.

I wanted to get up then and lift his coat from the sofa. I wanted to say brash and hearty things, the sort of things you say when you say good-bye to a friend, like, "See you next week," or, "Don't work too hard."

I wanted to say more than anything else, "Remember me to Monica," even though it would be absurd for I did not know Monica, but still nonetheless I wanted to say it to complete the circle of my purposeful respectability.

But I did and said none of these things.

Instead I sat looking at Paul, who looked at me until we could look at each other this way no longer in safety and without incident, and so he moved quietly forward, lifting my hand and kissing me gently upon the lips.

Try to remember how you made it from the sofa to the bedroom. You never can. Try and remember putting out the lights in the lounge, closing the bedroom door and taking off your clothes. Some things blot themselves out in your memory, why I do not know, for they are always, afterwards, the things you want to remember when you are scrabbling around for every tiny detail, trying to piece together the affair.

And yet you can remember, can't you, that first embrace, that moment when you sunk into each other's arms, holding each other like children for a long and perfect moment, breathing each other in, still and very peaceful, till you awoke, as if from a long sleep, and began to writhe, twisting heads back, seeking lips and eyes and breasts, seeking nervously and awkwardly and with excitement for that over which you will run a last slow reflective finger before setting it upon what has become the serious business of the night.

And now I want to ask Jo, sitting here at the table before me, Is it true then? Is it true what Michael said?

I want to ask her, head bent, finger stroking her forehead as she stares at the menu, Is he right?

I want to hear her scoff. I want to see her give me one of her shrugs of weariness, of disinterest. Who cares? It's the sort of thing Michael would say.

Instead she lowers the menu flat to the table, looking at me curiously.

"No, of course he's not right. We don't pick them because they're married. We pick them because they're the best of the bunch and if they're the best of the bunch they're bound to be married.

"They're the most attactive, the most confident, the most relaxed and easy and they can only be this way because of the wife at home, the woman who massages their ego and makes them feel good and provides them with the base they need from which to operate successfully.

"Compare them," she says, "with the single men of our age. Neurotic half-creatures. Miserable. Unable to look after themselves properly. Desperately in need of a woman.

"Really," she says, "men make the most terrible bachelors."

She picks up the menu and begins studying it again.

"Anyway, Rose," she says, "this all scarcely affects you. You're much too good to go stealing other women's husbands. And anyway you haven't got the time. Swotting away for God's sake like an eighteen-year-old. You'd never have time for an affair."

And then she raises her head again to summon the waiter, who appears almost immediately at her side, fidgeting with his pen and flicking his carbon paper, neatly and cleverly, between the pages of his notebook.

She begins to discuss with him in her friendly patronising fashion the merits of the butterscotch fudge-cake. Which is how the moment is lost, the moment when I might have said to her, "You're wrong, Jo. I've changed, Jo. I'm having an affair, Jo. With your brother, Paul, Jo. And it hurts, Jo. And I'm in pain, Jo. Help me, Jo. Help me."

"I'll have the profiteroles," I say.

6

"DAVID reminds me of someone," people say, puzzling, furrowing their brows.

"D. H. Lawrence," I tell them. "He looks like D. H. Lawrence."

But they say, "No. Can't be. I don't know what D. H. Lawrence looks like."

But they do, they do. Even though they may not realise it. Because he's always around, Lawrence. Another book about him. Another film. Another critical theory. Another corner of his life chipped away.

But always, at some time or another, that same picture.

The delicate young writer's face, set side-on like a cameo against the dark background, the absurdly small and feminine ear, the pale skin, the dark eyes, cool and wary, watching for the photographer's hand to drop outside the black stuff tent of the old plate-glass camera.

The hair short and neat and terribly vulnerable somehow, shining from a little natural greasiness or more likely from a little water hastily applied before arriving at the studio.

Mother's boy with a Mellor's man beard, all scrub from ear to jaw but ending in a sharp, puritanical jut, hiding the lips, the Lawrentian lips, the clue to the man, unsmiling, pursed a little, perhaps with the irritation of posing, but more likely with the constraint of holding compacted inside the sumptuous knowledge of superiority, of a destiny as priest and prophet and keeper of the key.

How extraordinary. To have such arrogance masked with such insidious diffidence, a diffidence that must have caught at Frieda's heart. A diffidence that I know has caught at Jennifer's.

It was bitterly cold the night we went to hear David read his poetry. His thin body seemed to nestle inside the green fatigues and combat jacket, and with his small wire-rimmed glasses slipping down his nose, he looked like a refugee from the sixties, like one of those hopelessly inadequate young men sent late on to a hopelessly foreign land to fight a hopelessly unwinnable war.

He read from a sheaf of dog-eared papers and pushed the glasses back up on his nose with a bony elegant finger.

His diffidence was most apparent in his voice, so that when he read his poetry the harsh violent language became somehow less offensive, appealing even, or touching, like the expression of bravado of a small and rather likeable young boy.

Glancing sideways at Jennifer, I could see immediately she was in love.

Her perfectly shaped full red lips were open slightly as she leaned forward to catch his words.

She sat upon the edge of the seat, her knees almost touching the chair in front, turning occasionally to glare at late-comers who scraped chairs or whispered, or to raise a hand to push back an insolent lock of hair which had fallen across her ear and which she feared might be preventing her from hearing the full effect of his voice.

We had gone actually, Jennifer and I, not to hear David but the famous novelist on the same literary bill. Probably I had partly gone to see Paul, for the glorious tutorials had started and I was already a little in love.

I remember I was put out to see Monica there looking exceptionally fine, her dark hair piled high on her head, looking a little gypsyish, her gold hoop earrings bright against the dark olive of her skin.

She stood behind the book stall, a soft black angora jumper falling off a glowing shoulder, a gathered skirt falling to the top of high leather boots.

I noticed the famous novelist give her a warm wide smile as he strode down the centre aisle on Paul's right hand, his own out-of-season tan making his face look even handsomer, his expensive mackintosh flying out behind him.

David, meanwhile, on long, loping legs ambled on Paul's left towards the stage, where they sat each side of the microphone while, between them, Paul made the introductions with genial, relaxed good humour.

The novelist, removing his mac to place it carelessly on the back of the chair, acknowledged his distinguished biography with a smile both self-deprecating and self-assured.

He smiled at Paul and at David, the satisfied smile of a man who knows his own talent and knows too that it is appreciated by the world.

Opposite him on an identical fold-up chair, David sat, one leg bent and lying with calculated nonchalance across the other, smiling back.

The smile was thin and amused and condescending and took in the mac and the tan and said he, the novelist, was welcome to such frivolities for he, the poet, preferred sterner, more puritanical stuff.

Monica stood square behind the many brightly coloured piles of the famous novelist's books while to her left, behind a pile of slim, rather dull-looking volumes, was a thin, gaunt figure, dressed all in black, a heavy belt bearing down upon her tiny hips and hollow navel.

A profusion of odd artifacts, crosses and rings and dangling pieces of metal, punctured her ears, and dozens of tiny silver bangles clinked on both arms as she touched constantly the pile of books, moving them each time an infinitesimal point nearer the centre of the table and the main thrust of the book-buying crowd.

Francie.

Unlike the famous novelist, whose queue stretched halfway up the hall and who sat, head bent, signing book after book, blindly and hurriedly like a candidate sitting an exam, David's line was tiny.

It ended, however, with Jennifer.

When I drew near I found her standing at his table looking down into his raised spectacles, which were twinkling with reflected light.

She turned the freshly signed volume before him, caressing it in her pretty pink-tipped fingers while talking in a soft, earnest voice of the stark, elemental nature of his work.

Below her, David nodded slowly but vigorously in appreciation of her words, the index finger working frantically on the bridge of his nose to keep the spectacles in place and Jennifer's loveliness in view.

It was then that I happened to glance at Francie and caught upon her face the most awful look of pain.

Behind the table, her hands rested lightly upon the green baize as she looked fixedly at the two of them, her whole body absolutely still.

Nothing moved either upon her face. It sat upon her shoulders like a head of alabaster, chiselled by a great sculptor who has learnt the supernatural art of etching upon cold, inanimate stone the warm, lively lines of human passion and suffering.

And then the statue moved. She looked away, deliberately it seemed to me, as if abruptly deciding that to keep looking and further distressing herself was fruitless.

She busied herself at the table, re-tidying unnecessarily the neat pile of David's books, drawing them together again with a brisk hard slap upon the baize and, after speaking a brief word to Monica, packing them away in a large box lying open upon the floor.

• • •

It was not long after that that David's name went up on a piece of card on the door of an empty room opposite Paul's. Beneath it a typewritten sheet gave students a brief résumé of the career of their new writer in residence and listed times when he would be available for consultation.

"The hours are good," I said, laughing to Jennifer as we stood reading it.

"He has to have time for his own work, Rose," she said primly, and I knew for certain then she was in love, for once she would have laughed at that.

A few days later we bumped into him outside his room. He was bending, his back to us, locking the door. A newspaper, freshly folded, poked out of a holed and frayed canvas shoulder bag.

Recognising Jennifer as he turned, he gave her a warm but wan smile.

"I've sat there for two hours," he said, "doing the crossword."

"Not the quick one, I trust," I said.

"Oh dear," said Jennifer, her lovely face falling into lines of the most delicious distraction.

"Oh dear," she said, hugging her pile of books to her breasts in sorrow.

Her eyes, gazing up into his, burned with distress.

And then they brightened.

"Wait," she cried. "Rose is working on a novel. I'm sure Rose would like your help. Wouldn't you, Rose?"

It was impossible to be angry with her, of course. It seemed churlish even to be annoyed. She was crestfallen, like a little girl who blurts out what she believes to be a wonderful plan only to be told by adults it is utterly unsuitable and she, being just a child, would have done better to have kept silent.

"I'm sorry, Rose," she said as we walked side by side to the library. "I didn't realise it was a secret."

"It isn't a secret," I said testily. "It's just not something I want to talk about, that's all."

"I just thought it must be so hard, working away on

something on your own every day. I thought it might be helpful for you to show it to someone."

"It's not ready to show to anyone. It might be rubbish for all I know."

"Oh no, I'm sure it's not, Rose. Not if you're writing it. No, I'm sure it's not.

"Anyway," she said, her voice losing its apologetic tone and re-gaining by stages some of its courage, "you'll have to show it to someone sometime you know, so why not David?"

That was when I noticed how she spoke the name "David."

She hesitated very slightly before she said it and then rolled it out lightly between her tiny white teeth as if trying out the sound of it.

And it sounded beautiful coming from her.

It became, moulded in her mouth, infinitely lovelier than the sum of its parts. She flattened her lips, drawing them back in a long "aaa," expelling the two "d's," at the beginning and at the end, very softly and gently, as if to herself, in private prayer, catching the "v" in the middle of her inside lip, like a child, lost in wonder and delight.

After that David began to appear wherever she was. He would materialise beside her as we sat drinking our coffee in the students' union, or in the foyer of the library as she entered arms full of books, or beside her car as she poked in her handbag for the keys.

Then one night I called round unexpectedly to borrow a book and there he was, stretched out upon the sofa reading, a glass of wine in his right hand, his old running shoes beside him on the floor.

Jennifer fluttered a little in the doorway, trying too hard to press a drink upon me.

"Actually David's here," she said unnecessarily.

He looked up from the sofa as we stood, the two of us, in the doorway, and he smiled, the cool, superior, silent smile I later found he always smiled at Jennifer's woman friends, the smile he would smile from the depths of the sofa, or later from the desk which she moved for him into the window bay, or sometimes from the kitchen where he would stand before the hob constructing spectacularly complicated curries which left the sink and the draining board packed with pans and bowls and kitchen utensils, the smile of the prodigal son, freshly robed and ringed and smelling the fatted calf, the "hello" smile that he smiles to his displaced, disgruntled, long-serving sisters.

Yes, David says they must always be honest with each other, he and Jennifer, which is why he told her early on about Francie.

He told her in such a way as to make her feel especially privileged that she had been selected to share his pain.

Having told her, he lifted his thin poet's hands to his face to remove his spectacles, as if in exhaustion, to pinch his eyes, to screw them tight closed and open them again to look deep into hers, to show her, lying there, packed behind the pebble lenses, all his pain and unhappiness.

"Oh, Rose," she says, the creamy skin around her beautiful almond eyes baggy and reddened with crying, "he's been so tired and upset. I'm just glad he's got me to talk to."

She called me. She said she wanted to try out a new soup or some such thing. But I knew she wanted to talk, especially when I arrived and found David nowhere in sight.

Now, in her favourite spot before the fire, she sips her wine like a disaster victim, taking strength before telling their story.

"It was so silly of me to get upset, Rose," she says.

"We had a terrible row but I see now he was right. He's never hidden anything from me. He told me about Francie, right at the beginning. And I know there's no reason to be jealous. Francie is his problem. Just something he has to work out. And until he does I just have to accept it.

"I've just got to handle it, Rose," she says, taking another sip of wine, her voice growing firmer and gaining with its strength an unattractive edge of self-satisfaction.

"I just have to be mature about it. Of course it upsets me, his going back at nights to Francie, but I mustn't let it show.

"Yes, I have to be adult about it," she says, firmly turning her little girl's eyes to me for approval of her resolution.

"To be honest," she goes on, lowering her voice a little at the seriousness of what she has to say, "I think he has a hell of a time with Francie. I mean it's terribly sad when a relationship comes to an end, but really you just have to accept it.

"And that's the trouble," she says sighing deeply, with the air of one forced to conclude she is rather hard done by, "Francie just can't accept it.

"No one has a right to hold on to someone who doesn't love them anymore. Really she has to see that."

I notice with surprise that her voice has grown prim and hectoring. Now she twirls her wine glass, pursing her lips in disapproval.

"As David says, she's completely illogical." Her voice as she says the word is full of awe flecked with horror, as though she is describing an unspeakable deviation.

"Sometimes she stands in the middle of the room weeping. Shaking and weeping. Sometimes she even screams. I mean it's so awful for him. There's nothing you can do with someone like that. It's all so unreasonable."

Her voice has grown cold now. Cold and conversational. The lovely eyes are quite clear again, the ugly redness and wrinkles quite disappeared.

Looking at her I feel a sudden intense stab of irritation.

"No it's not," I say. "You're quite wrong. It's not unreasonable at all. And it's certainly not illogical. Only a man would suggest that to stand in the middle of a room weeping and screaming when the person you love says he wants to leave you lacks reason or logic."

I am surprised at my feeling of gratification as I see her start back at the forceful, unsympathetic tone in my voice.

"Such behaviour may be annoying," I say, lecturing the lecturer. "It may even be distressing. There's an argument for saying it's extreme. But it certainly isn't illogical."

"Well," says Jennifer doubtfully, taken aback but trying desperately not to be seriously put out, "you may be right. But still," she raises her neat little chin in the air, "you can't hang on to someone who doesn't love you. I mean it's not as if they're married or anything."

"What's that got to do with anything?"

I can hear my own voice, which is belligerent and surprisingly unfriendly.

"And another thing. I really don't understand all this stuff about you having to be adult and mature. Frankly I think that's so much horse-shit. As far as I can see, since you love David and he won't give up Francie, it would be perfectly proper for you to stand in the middle of the room and scream and shout as well."

"Oh I couldn't do that," she says quickly. "Don't be silly. I'd be acting just like her. I mean he comes here to get away from all that."

"Oh and there we have it. The crunch. The guiding rule that keeps us in line and keeps our affairs all sweetness and light. Don't nag him or worry him or you'll sound just like his wife or in your case his live-in lover. What are we, Jennifer, a bunch of performing monkeys?"

Too late, too late I realise my mistake.

"'We,' Rose, 'we'?" she says, her eyes cloudy now with mystification.

"Yes, 'we,' Jennifer, 'we,'" I say with resignation. "I'm having an affair, Jennifer. With my tutor, Paul, Jennifer."

"Oh, Rose," she says, clapping her hands together in delight, all the hurt and confusion cleared from her face in an instant. "Oh that's wonderful. Oh I did always think when I heard you talking in the tutorials you were made for each other."

"Jennifer," I say, bemused and more than a little outraged at her joy, "Paul is a married man."

"Oh, yes of course, I know, I know," she says soothingly. "But he's not happily married is he? I mean we know that don't we? I mean you never see them together do you?"

She rushes on, her hands waving away in the air the lives of others.

"After all it's not as if you broke anything up is it? Things must have been going wrong before you got there. It's like David and me. I mean I feel sorry for Francie. Of course I do. But it's not my fault. That's the way things happen. It's the same for you and Monica. It's the same for both of us."

I am conscious of a huge rush of distaste as she couples us enthusiastically and airily together.

I know, with a shiver of dislike for the idea, that I don't want to be drawn together with her this way. I know I don't want to be the "you" to her "I" in her sharp, self-satisfied sentences.

But still she is speaking.

"Fancy, Rose," she says. "You of all people. And I always thought you were so different from the rest of us."

And then she looks at me, her eyes shifting kaleidoscopes of curiosity and surprise. And something else too. What is it? What is it? Yes, I have it. How did I not see it straight away? It is pleasure. Pure unmistakable pleasure.

A tiny pearl of pleasure lying between the curiosity and surprise, wrapped up in the suffocating folds of sisterly affection, shining out from those clear, uncompromising, girlish eyes, pleasure that Rose should be having an affair and can be seen now to be no longer different but, in this one all-important respect, just like all the rest.

"I'm so happy for you, Rose," she says.

7

a-dul + tery-y n., pl. + ter-ies. Voluntary sexual inter-
course between a married man or woman and partner
other than the legal spouse [C15 *adulterie*, altered (as
if directly from Latin *adulterium*) from C14 *avoutrie*,
via Old French from Latin *adulterium*, from adulter,
back formation from *adulterare*. See ADULTERATE.]

D O E S N ' T say much, does it really, the official
version? Doesn't really give you much of an idea what it's
all about. However, if you're interested, to "adulterate" is
to "debase with an inferior material." I like that. Being a
woman, I like that.

. . .

As I've said, I disapprove of adultery myself. I still do, although here I am an adulteress.

I live by one commandment, you see, not ten.

Written on my tablet of stone is: "Thou Shalt Not Make Another Woman Unhappy." And adultery, of course, by its very nature transgresses that.

My gut feeling, the feeling that floods my soul before I recover myself and remind myself of the need for a new spirit of detente, is that this world is an unhappy place for women, and the bulk of that unhappiness can still be laid directly at the feet of men.

Under these circumstances, any unhappiness caused by one woman to another seems gratuitous in the strongest sense of the word, absurdly, wilfully unnecessary.

A woman taken in adultery should be stoned. By other women.

And yet. And yet. And yet when his lips touched mine I did not say, as it so happens I have said a number of times in the past, "That was nice. Thank you. I have to tell you that I find you enormously attractive and I should very much like to go to bed with you, but the fact is you are married and that makes it impossible."

Sometimes, surprisingly, that is all that they want, this simple uncomplicated confirmation that years of marriage to one of the sex have not completely blunted their attraction to the others.

All they want is this little pat on the rump of their ego, this littlest of little bits on the side and, as a matter of fact, I'm a natural whore in that direction with a God-given talent for divining how meagre is the portion quite often required.

And yet. And yet. And yet I did not smile admiringly, regretfully, as it has become my custom so to smile in such circumstances, saying, "But of course I can't help caring about you very much and should like to think we could be friends," finishing the piece with, "Sometimes I think that friends are more important than lovers anyway," accompanied by a light, gay, slightly melancholy laugh.

And why did I say or do none of these things?

Because as his lips touched mine, circling my face, over and over very slowly from forehead to chin, I heard a small but pronounced click in my head closely followed by the sound of whirring.

It seemed then, with the feel of his lips soft on my face, as if I saw all my old notions of adultery playing on my closed eyelids, flickering in old-fashioned black and white, foolish and jerky and speeded up, spooling out onto the floor in an endless whispering slither.

Later, after our first love-making, lying together, the side of my face upon his chest, his chin upon my hair, two figures carved in stone, lying as if upon a tomb, he said, "You see there's something different about marriage, Rose."

He said, "You can't understand unless you've been married," and I remember his pomposity snagged at the back of my mind, but although I felt the pull, I registered it without scorn or distaste, for after all I was already a little in love and what is a little pomposity between those in love?

"You see," he said, "Monica and I aren't unhappy together. Far from it. Actually we get on very well. We exist quite happily in the same house."

"You go your way and she goes hers." Probably there was a hopeful note in my voice.

"No. Not at all."

He was staring up at the ceiling now. His eyes were open wide and he had the same exaggerated look of concentration upon his face as when he struggled to explain a difficult metaphysical concept or critical fine point to a student.

"No, it's true of course that we don't go out that much together, but that tends to be because we are both very busy people. But when we are alone in the house it's as if married life takes over, as if it slips back around you, like a blanket or a cloak."

"How long have you been married?"

"Nine years. And we lived together for five years before that."

"That's a long time."

"Yes, isn't it."

"But no children?"

"No."

"Why's that?"

"Just the way it happened."

"Would you like children?"

"I'm not sure. Hard to say when you've never had them. I've stopped thinking about it really."

"Would Monica?"

"Probably. Yes, I think so. Yes, she would."

"Have you had many affairs?"

"I don't know. What's 'many'?"

"'Faith, here's an equivocator.'"

"I don't know. Half a dozen or so."

"Or so? Or so?"

"I don't count."

"You count. Everybody counts."

"OK. Seven."

"That's 'many.'"

"Is it? Surely not? In fourteen years?"

"You're counting the first five years? Before you were even married?"

"You think it's doctoring the figures?"

"Yes, I think so. Shamelessly. When did you have your first affair?"

"Oh God. I can't remember."

"You can remember."

"Oh...I don't know...a couple of years after we were married."

"Two years?"

"If you say so."

"Two from nine is seven. Seven lovers in seven years. Am I this year's model?"

"And what about Monica?"

"What about her?"

"Has she had affairs?"

"Affairs, no. Affair, yes. One."

He spoke his name then, which made my eyes open wide with surprise. I turned from him, raising myself up on an elbow.

"Him! But he was here. A short time ago. The night Jennifer met David. You introduced him on the platform."

I was conscious of a sharp stab of disquiet, a jarring, a

spoiling of the moment and something else too, which, when I saw again the handsome face and the jaunty walk and the wide smile he threw at Monica, I knew was nothing more complicated than jealousy.

"Well yes. You sound surprised. But he was here you know. At the university. I said that. In my introduction."

"Yes of course, I'd forgotten. What was he doing again?"

"Writer in residence. Not much good actually. Students didn't go for him at all."

His voice which had grown confiding and gossipy smacked also of self-satisfaction.

"So what happened?"

"They met at a party. I was there. Monica and I were talking to him, and then later I saw the two of them talking alone. Didn't think much about it, but that's when it started. After that he began going into the bookshop. There's a little coffee shop there, you know?"

"Yes, I know."

"Anyway it developed into a full-blooded affair. There was a romantic weekend in the country when I thought she was with a woman friend..."

"So useful, woman friends."

"And then suddenly it was all over."

"Why?"

"I don't know. He was mad about her, apparently. Wanted her to go off with him. Things were looking good for him by then. His second novel was doing well. But for some reason she said 'no.'"

He sounded strangely unembarrassed, as though he enjoyed telling the tale. As though he was rather proud of her, undertaking an affair on her own like that with such creditable results. I recognised in his voice the odd blend of vanity and self-effacement with which I had heard him discuss a student of his who had done outstandingly well in the final exams.

"For some reason? Don't you know why she said 'no'?"

"No, not really. We talked about it of course, but still I don't really know. Sometimes when you talk, things just grow more and more confused. And Monica can be rather a confusing person."

"But you found out about the affair anyway?"

"Yes. But not then. A long time later. Quite recently actually. Last year. I'd been away for a month, lecturing in the States and I'd met...someone...while I was away. She rang me when I got home and Monica answered. We had a row. We'd both been drinking. She was ranting and raving. Saying she should have gone with him. I'd never seen her like that. Normally she keeps so calm whatever happens."

"Was it the night before your Conrad lecture?"

"Yes it was, as a matter of fact. How did you know?"

"You looked so awful. We all commented on it."

"Oh yes. You would. God, I hated you all that morning."

He ran a hand through my hair gently and apologetically, but although he smiled as he spoke, there was an edge to his voice as though the memory was still sharp and still just a little painful.

"There you were, all of you. Bright, eager women, sitting in the front row looking as though you were about to devour me. Sitting with your notebooks out and your pens ready. Looking at me as though I had all the answers. Hanging on to my every word. Soaking me up, sucking me in. God, how I hated you."

He reached to the bedside table then for a pack of cigarettes which he had taken from his jacket pocket as he undressed and carefully placed there, rather in the manner of a young man I remember from many years ago who took from another jacket a small alarm clock to place beside another bed for fear he should oversleep in the morning.

He lit one up, placing the match carefully in an ashtray he had brought, carefully too, into the bedroom.

"Actually," he said roguishly, "he wrote a novel about it."

"Yes," he said, "the third novel, if I remember. It's all about the affair."

He pronounced the title, good humour and the habitual self-deprecation teasing at the sides of his mouth.

"Good heavens. Don't you care? Aren't you even annoyed or embarrassed? Your wife spread over the pages of someone else's novel?"

"I don't look at it like that. As it happens it's a very good novel and, as a matter of fact, a very faithful portrait of

Monica. I believe I have to respect his integrity as a writer. And I have to accept that to a writer everything is fair game.

"Really," he said, turning aside to tap the ash off his cigarette, "Chekov said the whole thing so well with Trigorin."

Later I said what I'd been wanting to say all night.

I said, "Why do you stay together?" not as an idle enquiry but because I really wanted to know, because I thought his answer might throw some light on a whole way of living of which I knew nothing.

But he only said, "I don't know, really," disappointing me, and afterwards, "It's like I said, it's different when you're married" and other things, vague things like, "I'm not sure anyone knows. Affection, habit, laziness. Who knows?"

And then he said, "She's not like you, you know, Rose. You'd think she was the full-blooded feminist, the complete independent woman, especially having her own business and everything. But she's very vulnerable.

"She's not like you, Rose," he said.

"She's not like you, Rose," he said later, much later, laughing, laughing and kissing and taunting a little in the way lovers laugh and kiss and taunt after love, basking in their own wickedness.

"Monica would never ask so many impertinent questions on a first date."

And then he became serious again.

"She doesn't have your...self-reliance," he said, "your self-confidence. I can't imagine Monica on her own somehow. I know that in some strange way she does need me. That she couldn't manage without me."

The extraordinary thing is that it didn't upset me, all this. I wallowed in it as earlier I had wallowed in his love, rolling my body gently upon his and feeling every last inch of our skins adhere with the soft, sweet-smelling sweat of love.

"You are so sensuous, Rose," he said, his voice hushed in the silence, his eyes black in the darkness.

Who does not feel strong and fearless and in control with loving arms about them? And who at such a time will not embrace with enthusiasm the new-found responsibilities they see as thrust upon them with that love?

Who in such circumstances will resist the challenge of becoming the most benevolent, the most magnanimous, the most right-minded and well-principled adulteress in history?

"Paul," I said, urgently switching on the bedside light so that he might see my eyes, warm and womanly and full of concern, "I know you care about Monica. And I care too. Although I know that sounds crazy.

"Maybe it's true. Maybe I am...tougher somehow... than Monica. Perhaps I've had to be. I don't know.

"The fact is I want you. I want to make love to you. I believe we want each other. But I know we have to be careful about Monica. And I can handle that. I wouldn't want to hurt her any more than you would. In fact, being a woman myself, I should hate it if she was hurt. I should hate myself.

"I know whatever happens we must think of Monica."

He kissed me then, my alchemist, a long kiss, a grateful kiss, a kiss that melted the base metal of my misplaced self-admiration, bubbling it through love's old but trusty limbeck to turn it into the fool's gold of ill-founded, unwarranted self-confidence.

Yes, I felt so confident, so full of faith in myself, so calm and unafraid and unapprehensive about the future.

For what had I to be frightened of, I who live alone and am independent and known for my self-reliance and self-containment, I who need no one, I who am not like Monica?

8

YES, Paul's speciality is Conrad.

He sets examination questions like, "'But the honour, monsieur...the honour...that is real that is.' Discuss Conrad's concept of honour."

Yes, Paul sets examination questions on honour, but I do not think he understands the word as I do.

He says, "Of course honour is a disgraced ethic now. It belongs to the macho in our minds, to the Mafia, to Sicily, to South America."

He says, "Shame is the outward manifestation of honour.

To feel it you must know that everyone shares the same code as you.

"Honour," he says, "is all about reputation."

He stayed all night, one night, because Monica was away.

There was a sea-fret on the river, as thick as cotton wool. All night the fog horns went, a strange other world working away behind the mist while we made love.

Towards the dawn one sounded very loudly, waking me from the fitful sleep possessed of those sharing a bed who are more used to sleeping alone.

I slipped out from beneath the duvet and went to the window.

The dawn was piercing the mist with rays of bright white light. They struck an oil tanker passing smoothly and without shape or sound through the fog, the lights in its high white stern winking like diamonds set in a bodice of gauze.

I cried out, "Paul, Paul, look, look," and he woke with a start, half leaping from the bed, his face confused and a little disgruntled.

"There's your Conrad," I cried. "Look at it. Look at it. Never mind your theory. Never mind your symbols and your allegories. Just a ship passing through the mist at dawn. Such magic. Such mystery. It's enough, don't you see?"

He shook his head and ran a hand through his hair as if still trying to awaken himself and then pushed himself up on his hands to peer out of the window.

As the tanker slipped away, he settled back on the pillows.

"Rose," he said, wrinkling his brow and smiling, a little sadly I thought, "you look at things differently from me."

Sometimes only the simplest of words will do.

The truth is, I had never known such happiness.

I can remember the first time, can't you? When the world exploded suddenly into colour and life. The day he asked you to go for a walk in the park or for a ride on his motor-bike.

Well, that was how it was.

I felt loved. I felt wanted.

Tell me, what lights up the day better than that?

I took to phoning him to hear the way his lovely voice caressed my name.

"Rose," he would say, "how are you?" Although he knew how I was for he had examined me quite thoroughly the night before.

I took to calling upon him, unexpectedly, loving the way his face brightened as I entered and the way his hand swept his jacket from the back of his chair in a movement swift and easy and full of anticipation.

I took to asking, "A quick drink?" which, as every-one knows, is lover-speak for, "Come to bed with me, after first observing the formalities of a glass of wine or a meal, in the practised manner, pretending we do not divine our own singularly licentious inten-tions."

I took to searching out secret places, romantic places, for us to eat and drink, where the food and the wine would be sure of seducing him away from the things he thought he should be doing.

Which is how I found the lovely brasserie with the tiled floor and the square columns and the palms and the pian-ist with sad eyes seeing no one, playing a rosewood grand piano in the corner.

"If he plays 'As Time Goes By' we'll have another bottle of wine."

"Why don't we load the dice and ask him?"

"He looks as though he doesn't want to be disturbed."

"Is that your favourite song?"

"It's my favourite film. I cry every time still at the end."

"That's fantastic. You really are the new man, aren't you? Not ashamed to cry over a film."

"No. Not at all ashamed. I've always thought men should cry more, actually."

"Why don't they?"

"Because it's still not done, I suppose."
"Or because they can't find anything to cry over?"

Perhaps it was the wine that did it, or the music, or maybe we just lunched too long. But he said, "Come to Paris."
I had filled his glass from the second bottle, taking absurd pleasure in laying my hand back afterwards upon the table top, in curling it up, back to back with his, as lovers lie, back to back, in sleep, tired out after love.
He said, "I have to give a paper at a conference.
"It will do you good," he said, taking my hand and turning its finger-nails into his palm.
"It will give you a break. You work too hard," he said, his eyes twinkling and fatherly.
"Good food," he said, "good wine and..."
"Oh yes," I said. "I'll come."

And yet while so much has been gained, something also is being lost.
Here in the midst of all my happiness, something is leaking away, leaking away as we make love, with too little time, at hours not normally reserved for the purpose, early evening, for instance, before his night class, or at lunchtime or once, in the middle of the afternoon, when I should have been attending a lecture on contemporary women writers.
And struggling to give this something a name, I have found to my surprise it answers to "honour."
Yes, strange as it may seem, I believe now it is my honour that lies, a little off-colour and dispirited, plucking the bedclothes in vague distraction, while the rest of me leans itself upon an elbow to watch with a practised and self-confident smile as he re-clothes himself to turn his back and disappear out through the bedroom door.

Yes, Paul sets examination questions on honour, but I do not think he understands the word as I do. And I wonder now if Helen understands it, pressing with steady concentration her slice of lemon against the side of her long thin tea glass, here in the brasserie, at the very table where I sat with Paul, with the pianist tinkling away as before, sad and solitary and dignified in the corner.

What if I was to say to her now, "Helen, what about your
honour in this affair with Ray?" Would her head shoot up
in displeasure as she gave me a long outraged stare?

Would she look around her, nervously and furtively, as if
I had used an obscenity, inappropriate and out of context?
Would she say, "Really, Rose," dragging out the "really" in
disapproval, a moment later to recover herself, to become
embarrassed at her own indiscreet over-reaction, to lift the
silver-handled glass to her lips, gaining time and self-possession in the movement, then to look directly at me once
again, saying, with a small dismissive smile on her face,
"Really, Rose, don't be absurd"?

Yes, I think she would. I think she would do all of these
things. I think, therefore, I will not talk of honour to
Helen. And anyway, she has something else on her mind.

"I can't believe it. We've only been apart a couple of
months."

"Nearly six months now, Helen."

"He should have waited. For decency's sake."

"You mean like a period of official mourning?"

"This isn't funny, Rose. He's twenty years older than her.
He's forty you know."

"So what, if they're happy."

"It's ridiculous. A couple of weeks ago he's round three
nights a week making a nuisance of himself trying to fix
things around the house to get us back together again, and
now he's round nagging me to divorce and sell up so he can
get *married*."

"That's love."

"He's broke of course. Earning nothing on this little rag
he's working on."

Poor Helen. Someone has despoiled her honour but it
isn't Ray. It's Michael.

I see now she wanted Michael to do the honourable thing.
She wanted him to fight a duel. She wanted him to start his
own public relations business which would grow quietly but
steadily in stature until at some point in the plot it would
come to challenge Ray's. She wanted a battle in the business
pages. Which never will be. And now he's made her
ashamed. Simply by not making good. Poor Helen.

"What does it matter as long as he's happy?"

"Oh, he's happy all right. Are you kidding? Chasing after

fire-engines again like a junior reporter. Prancing around
with a little despoiled virgin on his arm."

"Helen," I say, moved to protest, "we were all despoiled
virgins once, you know."

"You don't know what it's like. Oh God, how she adores
him. She came with him to pick up Andy, which I don't
approve of at all. She trotted down the street with him,
falling off the kerb because she couldn't take her eyes off
him."

"What did Andy think of her?"

"What's that got to do with it?"

"Nothing. I just wondered, that's all."

"As a matter of fact he said he thought she was nice."

Her voice signals her distaste for the word. She pours
more hot water into the tea pot. The pianist edges slowly
and reluctantly into another tune, as if loath to leave the
last one.

"Helen," I say, crossing my arms in a firm and determined gesture, "why shouldn't Michael be happy with
someone else? You don't love him, at least not as a lover.
You haven't loved him for years. You can't do a big hurt
scene now."

"Why are you siding with him?"

"I'm not siding with him. If I was going to side with anyone, I'd side with you. I'd always side with a woman
against a man. It's the way I'm made."

It's a joke but she won't laugh. She won't look up and she
won't laugh. So I try again. Gently.

"Why shouldn't Michael fall in love and be happy? Even
if she's young. Even if it doesn't last. It's just as well he's
given up trying to get you back. I'm glad for him. Because
you don't want him back. He gets on your nerves. You
don't love him, Helen. He's put your nose out of joint by
finding someone else. But you don't love him."

"Whatever happens you had to get rid of Michael."

I see her body stiffen as the words leave my lips. She
raises her head and stares into the distance as if some ob-
ject has caught her attention and the conversation has become now of only secondary importance.

"What do you mean," she says slowly, her fingers very
tight and white around the glass, "'whatever happens'?"

Staring at the dreadful inflexibility of those fingers, I

see now that it is too late for hasty half-truths, it is too late for backpedalling or prevarication to try and undo the damage which has been done.

"I mean with whatever happens in the future. With you and Ray."

"And what do you think will happen?" She speaks the words calmly and very precisely, with a chilly smile upon her face.

"I think Ray won't leave the boys and I think I'm not telling you anything you don't already know. I think he adores them and I also think that life is not that bad with Sandra."

She has shifted her eyes. They look straight at me now, but there is a deadness in them, a distance, so that I feel as though I am shouting up to a stranger whose face I can see high up above me, staring out from behind grey stone battlements.

"I'm sure Ray loves you. I'm quite sure of that. But what Ray loves more than anything else, aside from the boys, is the business. And I think that's half what the love affair's about. After all, he's got you there, hasn't he, the woman he loves, sitting in the office next to him eight hours a day, or in your case more likely ten. Doing the thing he really loves best with a woman. Working.

"What do you talk about in bed, Helen? I'll bet it's work."

Let me tell you about Ray.

Ray is flash.

The more courageous and those who dislike him call him vulgar.

Jennifer, for instance.

"Really, Rose, I mean a *bright blue* Rolls-Royce."

Your mother would have called him a spiv.

Ray wears a chunky gold bracelet with a large "R" set into one of the links. It's too large for his rather small wrist and slips down all the time over the back of his hand as if determined to be seen, as if determined you shall not be fooled by the restraint of the dark business suit and the expensive hand-made shirt.

Ray has rich black hair, which shines without grease and which, however it is cut, at whatever over-priced unisex salon, still nonetheless flops undeterred across his dark olive forehead.

He is thin and small and even when standing quite still seems always to be on the move, as if a secondary image of him, another one besides the one before you, stands ducking and weaving, whistling through its teeth and insolently chewing gum.

For something about Ray seems to be permanently locked in the fifties. His expensive suits for some reason taper, as if by magic, upon his legs, and looking down at his feet it is always a surprise to see there the soft Italian leather shoes, rather than the shiny little winkle-pickers you expect to be curling their toes up at you.

Ray has parents still in a council house and a brother still in prison. He knows who recorded what and when. He'll sing it for you if you like. He'll tell you every cinema in the neighbourhood that once had double seats.

He's shot through with a rich will to succeed, with a seam of sharp, unashamed ambition which lets him be proud of the things that he loves, his business, his bracelet and his ten-year-old bright blue Rolls-Royce.

Ray is not a journalist. He cannot write copy good and fast as Michael can. But he can bounce ideas out nineteen to the dozen and talk contracts and deals so fast it takes your breath away. And he can take people to lunch and persuade them as they eat to do things they were convinced they were quite against doing.

All these things Michael never could do.

No, Ray cannot write, but he can buy the ones who can. And he can manage them better than anyone I know.

Ray would dig into his pocket and hand over to you a wad of notes uncounted if you asked him, waving away any worries of repayment.

And yet he hoards his money too, like a miser. He gives pay rises grudgingly, as if in agreeing to them he lets slip some highly prized personal principle.

His employees must go cap in hand to him for more money. They must sit before him, squirming and embarrassed and bemused and must ask him heart-rending questions such as: "But is this all you think I am worth?" at which he will appear genuinely upset and apologetic, saying such things as, "But I did not know you were unhappy" or, "You should have come to me before," and will then mention a figure, suitable but by no means over-generous, which will leave the employees speechless with gratitude and so humble and so dazed at their audacity that they will drop their glance at the door as they leave, thus missing the bright glint of amusement in Ray's eyes as he grasps their hand and says, "Remember, come and see me anytime... anytime at all you are unhappy."

Yes, Ray is flash. But he is also very clever. And like many of those who are very clever, he likes to play the hick.

He likes to pretend he is less intelligent than he really is. For instance he used to slap Michael on the back and tell everyone that he, Michael, was the brains of the business. He did it once with great audacity, with eyes clear and lips twitching, at the bar after Michael, the director, had gone like a humble clerk to ask for more money.

Yes, Ray liked to slap Michael on the back and tell us it was all down to Michael. But nobody was fooled.

As at Michael's farewell. Nobody was fooled.

Helen is lifting her bag from the floor, her expensive leather organiser bag with its pockets for everything, her keys and her purse and her chequebook.

The pianist is playing "As Time Goes By," eyes lowered, coffee gone cold upon the piano-top.

Perhaps it is the music that does it.

"I'm sorry, Helen," I say. "I'm sorry if I hurt you. The fact is I know how it feels. I'm having an affair myself, with Paul. My tutor. With Jo's brother, Paul."

She was folding a soft mohair scarf around her neck. Now she stands stock-still beside the table. I can see now that of all I have said, this one thing should not have been spoken.

I see now that, of all things, Helen does not wish me, like her, to be having an affair.

She allowed the words I spoke earlier on the understanding that they were being spoken by someone unlike herself, someone trustworthy by reason of her virtue, someone above reproach, someone who had remained strong where she had weakened.

What I said hurt her and yet in some way she wanted to

hear it. She wished the facts to be stated. She wished to hear told what she should not be doing even though she was quite certain she would continue to do it.

She trusted me when she let me speak, and now she feels betrayed.

She sweeps away from the table so that I must grab my coat and bag quickly to follow her and must half run to keep up with her as she strides down through the tables to the glass doors and out onto the street.

Half hopping in an awkward sideways motion beside her, I insist on telling her about Paul, how it started, how it continues, where we go to make love.

"That's how I found the brasserie, Helen," I say.

I know she does not want to hear. She would like to put her hands over her ears. She quickens her step still more so that my breath comes in pants as I tell her the times and the places and the silly sacrilegious details.

"We're going to Paris, Helen," I say.

Nearing the car, she reaches into her handbag for the keys. But they are not where they should be, and she has to scrabble desperately around in the labyrinth of pockets.

"Of course I feel terrible about Monica," I say. "I think about her a lot. I feel so sorry for her. You must feel the same about Sandra. It spoils everything, doesn't it. Them being married."

Beside the car now, she turns her back on me deliberately, continuing to rifle in the bag for the lost keys.

"It's our honour, Helen," I say, clutching her arm. "I tried to figure out what it was I felt was being lost and I think now it's our honour."

She has found the key now and is poking it frantically and ineffectually at the lock, scratching the paintwork on the door as she does so.

It strikes the metal again and again as she fumbles with panic and the passionate need to get away, until at last the door gives and she is free of me and inside the car.

I can see her now in the darkness, breathing very deeply behind the window as she searches for the ignition. The small interval calms her, and as she switches on the lights, I can see the panic is subsiding.

She starts the car up and reverses it out slowly, to drive it away. Exhaust comes out in a great cloud as she presses down hard on the accelerator, the car still stationary before me. And then she winds down the window, light from a streetlamp full on her face.

"At least they've no children, Rose," she says, leaning out calmly towards me.

"You're lucky in that. If he loves you there's no reason for him not to leave Monica."

I know that it will be three of us at the cinema now, or maybe four. Perhaps Helen and Jennifer and Jo at the theatre or maybe Helen and Jennifer and Rose. But never Helen and Rose out together, alone.

For Helen does not wish to be coupled to me in adultery as I did not wish to be coupled to Jennifer.

Helen does not want to sit beside me in the intimacy of a theatre, does not wish to rub her pain against mine in the darkness of a film. Helen does not wish to sit across the table from me in a restaurant, seeing the hurt in her own eyes reflected in mine.

Helen does not want to join me in suffocating girl talk, exchanging confidences about the days he could not make it, the nights when he did not arrive.

No, Helen does not want our friendship to be grounded on an interminable and intimate exchange of the slings and arrows of adulterous love.

Actually I knew all about Michael and his new love before she told me. I bumped into him in the brasserie the day I went there with Paul.

I was weaving a little tipsily back from the toilet when he appeared from behind a column.

"Only lovers and old ladies use tea-rooms in the afternoon, Michael," I said gaily.

"I'm in the first group. How about you?" he said, his eyes flicking to a table where a young girl was sitting.

"Me, I'm with an old lady," I said, suddenly glad that Paul was hidden away behind a graceful arc of palm.

"Oh really, do I know her?" said Michael.

"No, I don't think so," I said, wanting now to be away from him and trying to push past.

"You're blushing, Rose, you're blushing," he said, in the boozy, buffoonish middle-aged man's voice which I hated.

"Who can she be, this old lady who makes you so red? Don't tell me she's married, Rose, and that's why you're blushing? Not you, Rose, as well."

"You're a scream, Michael," I said through lips stiff with smiling.

"Not you as well, Rose," he said again. "You're all at it, aren't you? My dear wife Helen, and then Jo, and now you."

"You forgot Jennifer," I said, the smile quite gone from my face.

"And Jennifer too," he drawled, jerking back in mock amazement.

"In a manner of speaking," I said.

"My goodness," said Michael, moving aside to let me pass, "you must have so much to talk about. You should form a club, you women. A Women's Adultery Association. With outings and meetings."

"You could bring out a handbook," he said.

And that's when it happened, that first tiny quiver in reality, that small passing away, that momentary blotting-out of the brightness of the sun.

It dulled for an instant the ornate glory of the art deco mirrors. It took the sheen off the potted palms and made the piano tinkle a little emptily and jangle a handful of notes out of tune.

But then suddenly everything was bright again and melodic, and failing to put a name to the dip, I dismissed it from my mind.

And it was only later, when it happened again, when I felt once more that sinking, that I spotted the fragment of what had fallen away, and stooping to lift it found it to be honour.

And was surprised, not that I had lost it but that I had ever had it to lose and more, that it should have been before, of all people, Michael that I felt its first falling away.

Yes, I was surprised that it should have been Michael who, oddly, made me ashamed, Michael before whom I felt the absurd diminishing of reputation, Michael in whom I failed to recognise the first reflections of my own lost honour, Michael who I know for a fact does not share the same code as myself.

9

"YOU'RE all at it, aren't you," Michael said. "My dear wife Helen, and then Jo, and now you."

I'm sorry Michael knows about Jo and Martin.

Of course Martin is indiscreet. His eyes, for instance, follow her too obviously around the room. But then Jo's affection is amiable and unaffected in public, the sort that might pertain between a loyal party member and her MP, and I always thought this rather put outsiders off the scent.

Yet I suppose I should not be surprised, knowing Michael as I do.

Scandal, the tit-bits and garnishes of other people's lives, has always been meat and drink to Michael.

In the old days he was, after all, what they call a good reporter, settling down to the humble mess of pottage that was someone else's marriage with an innocent, enthusiastic appetite.

I can see, even as she approaches in the distance, that something is wrong. She is hurrying and she never hurries. Even in a rush she seems to amble, her long legs striding, bouncing her long pear-shaped breasts gently as she walks.

But now she hurries, her hands jammed into the pockets of her ski-jacket, diving in sharp irritated movements between the indecisions of the parcel-laden late night shoppers, her lips forming in silent curses.

"Look, let's scrap the cinema. Do you mind?"

The "Do you mind?" is rhetorical. A formality. Now in the corner of a garish and unsuitable pub nearby, she waits for me to take the first sip of my drink, pushing a small dish of peanuts around the table with a thin and restive finger.

"Margaret's told Martin she wants a divorce. She knows all about us." She takes a packet of cigarettes and throws them carelessly down on the table.

"Really," she says, "it's so inconvenient."

Jo never carries a handbag.

Chequebook, credit cards, purse and cigarettes are secreted about her person in many pockets like a man.

At work she carries a large battered brief-case, identical to the one her brother carries, given upon graduation by the same father.

Margaret, though, carries a handbag all the time as if in some way her life depended upon it.

When I see it hanging off her shoulder, I feel the tears prick behind my eyes.

There is something so vulnerable about a woman's handbag, the way she clutches it to herself, as if in losing it she might lose, too, her identity, as if contained inside it is everything she is.

To see a stolen handbag cast away, lying gaping on the

ground or in a hedge, its petty personal contents strewn
around, is to be the unhappy witness of a small outrage.

To see it lying, the survivor, by one new dead is almost
more than the heart can bear.

Margaret's shoulder bag is soft and pouchy and made of
Spanish leather, bought on holiday, with Martin, before
there were children.

It is battered now, battered as Jo's brief-case. One buckled strap is mended, crudely sewn together, a piece of
thread left hanging.

It bulges at the seams, straining with the paperwork of a
wife and mother, appointment cards, bills paid/unpaid, library tickets, dry-cleaning slips, the car insurance, cou-
pons cut out carefully, always off the next purchase and
therefore never used, lists of groceries and Christmas
cards, of things to do, agendas for peace group meetings
and parent-teacher groups, newspaper cuttings, the blouse
she never sent for, old photographs, the drawing Danny did
for her, his first major work, entitled "Mummy Crying."

One day Margaret cannot find a prescription form she
slipped into the bag only minutes before.

She drops her head down onto the steering wheel and
howls, the howl of a defeated animal, silencing the children in the back seat.

Her life has disappeared without trace into her own
handbag, submerged beneath the slurry of injunctions, instructions, reminders and remembrances of other people's
lives.

"I don't know what came over her," he said to me, his
face a study in fatherly outrage. "Scared the hell out of
Danny.

"I made a joke of it," he said, magnanimous now. "I said,
'I'm not surprised you couldn't find it in there.' I said, 'I
hope I'm cast up on a desert island with you. We'll have
everything as long as you have your handbag.

"'We'll have everything,' I said, 'including the gramo-
phone and eight records.'"

He smiled as he remembered.

"You're such a shit, Martin," I said.

• • •

Jo carries cigarettes in one of her pockets but never a lighter. Yet she seldom buys matches. Asked for matches by Jo, barmen will almost invariably reach behind them and toss a packet to her, shaking their heads as she holds out some money.

Often, though, she does what she is doing now, turns to the man sitting next to her who is smoking and picks up his matches lying upon the table, saying, "May I?" while already removing one from his box and striking it against the side before him with her strong sensuous fingers.

"Why, goddamn it," she says. "Why does it have to happen now?"

"What's so special about now?"

"I'm in for a seat. I'm in for *the* seat. I can't believe it. I can't believe such good luck."

Her face has lost altogether the loose expression of boredom bordering on irritation which it wears for so much of the time. Instead it is tight and animated. She leans forward, inhaling hard on her cigarette.

"They've got to give me this one. There's no way they can get out of it this time.

"No one but no one can be better for this seat than me," she says, pronouncing the name in triumph.

"My God. Your home town. How come?"

"He's retiring."

She says his name, tossing it aside with the match into the ashtray.

"Usual story. Lazy right-winger who likes to blame the left for all his troubles. He's been persuaded to retire come the election to avoid a messy de-selection. He has a good excuse. His wife is ill. I had a call to say I'm on the short list. I have to be favourite. Everyone's betting on June now for the election so they'll be selecting as soon as possible. I'm going down at the end of the week to stay with the folks and see the lie of the land."

"Is it a safe seat?"

"It was before he got it, but he's let the votes slip away over the years."

"Who else is in for it?"

"A local councillor, dull as ditchwater, a militant social worker, and a London barrister far too smart for his own good."

"All men."

"All men."

"So you're the token woman."

"No." She says "no" angrily, grinding the cigarette half smoked into the ashtray. "Not this time.

"This time I'm not a token anything."

"Look," she says as if rehearsing to me, as she has rehearsed to herself, all the evidence in the case, "my credentials are impeccable. No one's better than me at patching up squabbles between the right and the left. I did it here for Christ's sake. And this time it's not a sponsored seat. This time we don't have the union putting in their own. On top of that it's my home patch. I was born and brought up down there. I joined the Young Socialists there. And then of course there's my father."

You won't know Jo but you'd know her father. A Socialist. Of the old school. A benign academic with an exemplary war record. Met Jo's mother in the Resistance in France. Undismissible. Even by the right. Respected. Admired. Appears on television. Writes in the *Times*.

"I mean it's got to help, the old man waving his walking stick around the home patch beside me.

"I've got everything going for me. The only fly in the ointment is Margaret."

"What you don't need right now is a scandal?"

"What I need is an impeccable private life, an impeccable façade to cover my impeccable credentials."

"Bye-bye, Martin."

"Exactly."

"But will that be enough?"

"I'm sure of it. Margaret doesn't want a divorce. She just wants to frighten him. She wants him back. Mad woman. It's just blackmail. This all blew up when Martin was stupid enough to let slip about the seat.

"I've told him," she says, reaching for another cigarette and again for the matches, "it's all up to him. He's got to patch it up. He's got to play the happily married man and make her think he means it. I've told him it's his seat on the line, too. His little majority would disappear without trace into the black hole of a mucky divorce case."

"How did she know? About you and Martin."

"She's not stupid. She must have guessed. I've always said God knows why she stayed with him. And then he came back one night pissed as usual and blurted it all out in a weepy confession. God, can't you just hear him?"

Disgust spreads across her face as she taps an angry finger on the cigarette.

"So what about Martin?"

"What about him?"

"I mean what does he think about it?"

"Him!" Her voice rises in derision.

"It doesn't matter what he thinks. He can't put half a dozen coherent words together at the moment. One moment he's weeping on my shoulder, saying of course it's all over and he has to make a go of it with Margaret, the next he's day-dreaming about lustful nights in London when I'm elected.

"Frankly," she says, "Margaret can have him. I'm fed up with him anyway. He's not a good enough fuck to lose a seat for."

The man at the next table wants his matches back. She tosses them lightly onto the table with a smile, vague and automatic. The toss more than the smile attracts him.

He is in his forties, a businessman, drinking with colleagues from the office. He is quieter than they. Thinks himself better. More intelligent, less uncouth, less unliberated. He is married and loves his wife but fears he is growing old before his time. Jo attracts him. He cannot handle her and he knows it but, with several drinks inside him, he is willing to risk almost certain humiliation to try.

He is moving very slightly towards her when she says, "Let's get the fuck out of here."

Strangely the shock of her language adds to her attraction. He wants to stop her going. He tries to think of something to say. But the fierce masculine way she shoots her coins and notes from the table top into her hand and stuffs them, without regard, into a pocket silences the words before they are shaped.

I see his eyes rise to the mirror on the wall facing him above the heads of his colleagues. In it he sees an image of himself, undistinguished, sandy-haired and balding. His eyes hold his own for a moment and then he turns his attention back, a shade gratefully now, to his colleagues.

In the car I say, "You despise Martin, really, don't you."

It makes her angry. She says, "Really, Rose. You want to make everything so simple. Margaret loves Martin and I despise him. She's the madonna of the piece and I'm the she-devil. Everything has to be so black and white with you."

"It's true though. You do despise him."

"No." It is not a denial. Just a word, drawn out, thoughtfully, while she thinks what she means.

"I like him actually. It's true he bores me sometimes but then so do all men. Men are essentially rather dull. Even the brightest and the best. It's part of their nature. If you like them you have to put up with it."

"Do you think it's right? Feminists being adulteresses?"

"I'm not." Her voice is surprisingly sharp.

"An adulteress commits adultery with someone other than her husband. I have no husband. I cannot by definition be an adulteress."

"That's a technicality surely?"

"Not at all. I have no partner. I'm the innocent party. It's not my fault if the man I choose to go to bed with has a tawdry unsatisfactory little marriage running along on the side."

"But a woman who has an affair with a married man knows she's making another woman unhappy."

"Not necessarily. Your problem, Rose, is that you have to be so dramatic about everything. Not all wives are weeping whey-faced at home because their husbands are out with another woman. Some of them are probably quite glad to be rid of him. As long as he pays the bills why should they care? They've got the house and car and the kids. What more can they want?"

"That's awful. That's so awful. That's so terribly patronising to other women."

"Oh for God's sake, Rose."

She is screwing her head round to park the car. I can hear the annoyance in her voice but cannot see her face.

"You really do have this ridiculously romantic view of your own sex.

"Really your imagination quite runs wild faced with the alleged agonies and travails of the married woman."

He says to me urgently, standing at the bar, a cigarette to his lips, watching Jo at the farther end of the room, "Look, I know I'm a bastard."

I like Martin. I've always liked Martin. Martin, tall and grey-haired from a boy, handsome in a big-bellied way, overbearing sometimes certainly, especially when drunk, but lovable enough for you to be unoffended when he puts a large affectionate paw around your shoulders. Martin. Big foolish old bear Martin.

"I know I'm a bastard," he says, the "bastard" flat and hard and northern. "I look at the facts of the case and I know I'm a bastard. All I can say is it doesn't feel that way."

He runs a hand through his hair, straining it back from his forehead.

"I can't look at her sometimes," he says. "I'm so ashamed. She closes the bathroom door now and locks it when I'm around. I know what I'm ashamed of but what's she ashamed of, that's what I'd like to know."

"Of losing your love. Of not being attractive enough to keep you and all those other things women have been taught to be ashamed of."

"But it's not true. This thing with Jo. It has nothing to do with my marriage. It doesn't affect my love for Margaret. She's my wife. The mother of my children. I love her in a special way. Nothing can ever change that."

"Some consolation," I say to his back, "this special way."

He has turned to call to the barman. "No more for me, Martin," I say, but he orders anyway as if he does not hear.

"She despises me, of course, I know that," he says, handing me my drink.

"She's more intelligent than me. I accept that. I know there are others. I'm just a... convenience." He lingers a little over the word, smiling to himself. "And I know she despises me sometimes."

"This is crap, Martin. I don't want to hear it. She has no reason to despise you."

I'm angry at him and raise my voice, but he goes on, in soliloquy, as if only for himself, as if unaware anyone is listening.

"It's her voice I love more than anything else," he says.

"Don't tell me. Chock full of the good things in life, full of class and confidence and a congenital understanding of good wines. Full of books and music and all the things we never had. Full of a first-class education. Full of a Socialist academic father and a French Resistance mother..."

"How did you know that?"

He breaks in on me, looking puzzled and unsettled.

"Here's to the bourgeoisie, Martin," I say, raising my glass to him.

"Here's to the bourgeoisie."

Heads together now at a table at the end of the bar, they attempt, unsuccessfully, some privacy. For party workers, aware of no special occasion, approach them constantly.

Each time the pair wave them to a seat exchanging pleasantries, in an easy manner, as if the disturbance was of no consequence, as if they talked, heads together like this, of constituency business, or party strategy, or the date of the election.

And now the barman calls "Drink up now" and "Time to go." She bends her head, talking urgently all the while, keeping a friendly undisturbed smile upon her face. Martin meanwhile slumps in his chair, his eyes fixed upon his hand, which is grasped around a glass that he turns slowly and belligerently upon the table.

Lifting her coat from the chair beside him, she asks him a question, but he will not answer or even look at her, merely shakes his head.

Instead he stretches his legs below the table, as if very tired, and raises the glass with its few drops of whisky slowly and deliberately to his lips.

He raises it as though he had all the time in the world, as if the barman were not now calling "Drink up now *please*" in a voice louder and more hostile than before, as if people did not pass him and slap him on the back and say "'night, Martin" and "Cheers, Martin," as if a woman were not at that moment asking him a question and, not receiving an answer, would not then remove herself from his table, and to all intents and purposes, remove herself also from his life.

"He's drunk," she says contemptuously. "I've told him he should have a lift with me but he won't even answer. So let him get done for drunk driving. What do I care?"

At the door I throw a last look at Martin.

He sits exactly as before, unmoving, his eyes still fixed upon his glass. But the barman is beside him now, emptying the ashtray into a can. He is talking to Martin. He is trying to persuade him to leave but he's trying to persuade him without being unpleasant. For they are old friends and he does not wish to be brusque.

In the car going home I say, "Do you think I'm romantic then? Over women?"

"Really, Rose, I don't know."

Her voice is sharp. She was thinking deeply about something, staring straight ahead over the wheel, and I disturbed her. A small pucker of irritation forms between her eyebrows as she collects her thoughts against her will.

"You do take a high moral tone sometimes. I offend you because I have affairs, but it's not so much the affairs themselves you don't like but my attitude. You disapprove of me because I refuse to feel bad about them. But let's face it, given my age and the unavailability of single men, not to mention their inferior quality, I really have no choice. If I want sex, and I do, I have to accept that the men will be married."

She braces herself against the back of the seat and relaxes, her hands becoming limp on the wheel.

"You see the thing is, Rose, it's easy for you to be good because you're not that bothered about sex. I mean look at you, sitting at home all buttoned up with your books like a little nun."

Her voice has lowered a tone and is warmer now and inoffensive.

She throws a sideways glance at me.

"I mean when was the last time you actually went to bed with someone, for God's sake?" she says, laughing.

"The day before yesterday, actually."

"Good heavens." She starts back in her seat in mock surprise.

"You've been keeping this one a secret. Anyone I know?"

"Yes, someone you know quite well, actually. Your brother Paul, actually."

And now her surprise is real. I see it in the wideness of her eyes turned to me in the light of a passing streetlamp. And something else I see too, something half-hidden in the surprise, a sharp stab of displeasure glimpsed and then gone, gleaming in the soft stuff of her amiability like the blade of a knife.

"Well, well. My baby brother. My goodness me. And how long has this been going on?"

The laughter is light and amused, the laughter of one who has regained, after a momentary lapse, a customary self-possession. And I wish I had not told her now. I wish the words had not been said. They seem wasted and wilful and grossly unsuitable, and I know now, with a passion, that I do not wish to discuss this brother with this sister.

I turn my face to the darkness beyond the window, answering her slowly like a sulky child.

"About a month or so."

"And have you found out yet that beneath that unassuming exterior he's hopelessly arrogant and utterly selfish? He really is the centre of his own universe, you know."

She is brisk now and friendly. Her voice rakes through my mind, dragging at my discomfort, overturning it, exposing it to the air.

"We're going to Paris," I say dully, in the voice of one who, found guilty, has decided to tell all.

"He's out of your league," she says crisply, her eyes on the mirror as she changes gear and turns the wheel with her familiar assured and slightly flamboyant gestures.

"He'll never leave Monica, you know."

"I never assumed that he would."

"Poor old Monica," she says, shaking her head with a snort of a laugh as she roars the car into top gear. "Putting up with him all these years.

"You know about what's-his-name, the writer? God knows why she didn't go with him."

"Why didn't she?"

"Who knows. We've never been close, Monica and I. We don't socialise. Never have. They've been to the odd party of mine. Frankly I can never think of anything to talk to her about. We exchange obscure kitchen utensils at Christmas and birthdays but that's about the limit of our relationship."

There is silence for a moment, and when she begins talking again, it is as if she is musing out loud.

"He'll never leave her. He's just like Martin. They're all the same. They all need to be looked after. Once they've had a wife they can't manage on their own. I mean look at the ones who do get divorced. They go and marry exactly the same sort of woman again. Once you've wiped your feet on a doormat, of course you miss it. Look at Martin. He wouldn't know how to pay the gas bill or tax the car. Probably doesn't know where the kids go to school or if he takes sugar in his tea. He'd be crazy to lose Margaret. That's what I told him tonight. I mean who the hell would look after him if she went?"

She is in full flow now. I lean my head against the window. I can see the subject of Paul and me has slipped from her mind, pushed aside by her own more pressing concerns.

"Yes, I told him he may fuck things up for himself but he's not fucking them up for me. I have to get this seat. This is my last chance. I'm thirty-seven now. They don't like women over forty, although they deny it, of course, but it's true. I have to do it this time. And goddamn it, I deserve this seat. I've given a good twenty years of my life massaging their bloody male egos for the cause, not to mention what I did here.

"It's true what Martin says. I did get him in. I patched up the splits in the party for him. I got them all out and onto the doorsteps. I got the press out for him. Even told him what to say sometimes.

"It's true what he says when he's pissed," she says, squirming back in the seat in self-satisfaction. "He couldn't have done it without me. It's me that won the election for Martin."

Personally, I think she's wrong.

Personally, I've always thought it was Danny who pushed Martin past the post.

Danny, protruding from Margaret's stomach, leading the way as she stumped her way around the constituency, a mountain, moving slow and tired but smiling. Womanfully.

Danny, a gift from the patron saint of MPs, born two weeks premature, five days before the election.

Danny, born hale and hearty, a little crumpled but with a smile all ready for the cameras.

Danny, who came into the world looking for his father, who couldn't be found because he was still out somewhere, canvassing, although it was late, and who was preaching to the converted as it happened, discussing the need for disarmament, beneath the faded Russian flag which serves as a quilt on the mattress on the floor which has always been Jo's double bed.

10

 **V I R G I N I A** Woolf said life is not a series of carriage lamps symmetrically arranged.

But then Virginia Woolf had never seen The Green.

At the time, the estate agents were pleased to announce the release for sale of an exclusive development of eight executive homes of elegance and distinction, fitted out to an exceptionally high standard, with four bedrooms, including one with *en suite* bathroom, luxury fitted kitchen/breakfast room with adjoining utility room, spacious lounge and walk-through dining area featuring natural stone fireplace and large picture window, the homes sited around a central landscaped green, giving the development a delightful country feel.

Michael and Helen bought Number Five after their accountant persuaded them they needed a larger mortgage. Number Five was the last to sell, for no good reason, since all the houses were exactly alike, each with its lamp at the door, its two puny saplings shrinking on the lawn and its massive picture window staring out at the night, like the screen of a drive-in movie.

Tonight the undrawn curtains at Number Five, formerly Helen and Michael's but now just Helen's, reveal the truth about parties. That they all look the same from the outside.

Guests perch upon the arms of chairs and spindly barstools and lounge against the wrought iron work of the open-plan stairs, as if intent upon discovering the most awkward and uncomfortable positions in the house, clinging at the same time to the perimeters of the rooms as if alert to the possibility of being asked to disport themselves in some unacceptably sociable fashion.

"Why won't they *dance,*" Helen hisses in an agony of desperation.

They won't dance because the music does not invite them to do so.

It escapes, thin and reedy and unexciting, from a radio cassette machine which is the only source of music in the house since Helen agreed to give up the stereo in exchange for the fridge and the washing machine.

Actually Michael offered, magnanimously I thought, to bring it back for the party, but Helen airily declined, saying, "It's OK, Michael. The tape will do. It'll sound fine once everyone has a few drinks inside them."

Sadly, though, the guests are drinking with studied moderation. For the party has about it an unhappy still-born air, and the guests, divining this, are plotting ways of escape. The more brazen have already sidled shamelessly towards the hall where they feign animation, spinning out their drinks while relishing the prospect of an early night.

For the music, playing pluckily away in the corner, is a symptom, not the source, of the sickness from which the evening is suffering.

It pipes a Last Post, a tinny valediction for enjoyment, expiring slowly and painfully from the suffocating responsibility of making this, Helen's first party on her own, a rip-roaring success.

One Saturday night in the first heady months when Helen and Michael and all the other young couples had not long moved in, there was a joint party, a barbecue, held one balmy late summer evening on the green itself. There's a small patch of brown still where the grass has since steadfastly and superstitiously refused to grow.

For the evening was a complete disaster, against all the odds since the guest list set new standards in social homogeneity.

However contrary to all expectations, the friends of the solicitor at Number Seven fell out with those of the estate agent at Number Three, while the regional sales manager for the domestic appliance firm at Number Six was so far from seeing eye-to-eye with the founder of the micro-electronics firm (Queen's Award to Industry 1979) at Number Two that he punched him in the mouth at three o'clock in the morning.

Michael, who found the wife of the former in a horizontal embrace with the latter on a pile of carpets in the garage at Number Four, thought this the more likely source of the disagreement rather than the one given, which was the government's handling of the money supply.

Anyway, there were no more joint parties after that. They hold their parties separately now, watching those to which they are not invited through the wide screen of the picture window.

Jennifer is here.

Helen called her to invite her and said, "Tell Rose, would you, and save me a call."

Yes, Jennifer is here, with David of course, sitting at his feet, one loving arm draped across his freshly ironed fatigues.

Her voice is a gentle murmuring adagio of questions and admiring assents at his answers.

As he speaks he rolls a cigarette with his thin, delicate fingers, his long legs stretched into the natural stone fireplace which glowers like a granite cliff face along one wall, dwarfing the attempts at merriment from the feeble little fire.

I am here. But not Paul. Of course, not Paul.

There is a code, nonetheless rigid for being unwritten, that says you do not invite your married lover to your girl friend's party, particularly since it is almost certain he will not come.

Next time you are at a party, conduct a quick straw poll of its intelligent, presentable unaccompanied women, and you will find a sizeable percentage there alone, courtesy of a married lover.

Notice their restrained and dignified demeanour, how, for instance, their evening seems to adhere to a pre-deter-mined time-table. They are pre-set. They wash and dry to order. It is thanks to them the glasses never run out. Watch them as they clear away, discreetly, the dirty plates and restore the ravished food table. See them move silent and unnoticed among the other guests, lifting here a burn-ing cigarette about to set the house alight, there a broken glass beneath the heel of a barefoot dancer. Observe them fetch the coats for departing guests and say good-bye for the hostess, busy in the kitchen kissing someone else's husband.

Mark, most important of all, how these modern Cinder-ellas manage to leave a lingering impression of having been the life and soul of the party, of having thoroughly enjoyed themselves, when they have in fact spent the en-tire evening with one eye on the clock, willing its leaden hands to move while warding off the tedium with their self-imposed domestic duties.

Helen has invited Ray and Sandra and Michael and Kathy. For the same reason. Because she thought she should. Because she has it in her mind that this is the way it is done, this being civilised, this acting like an adult, this treating everything that has happened as if it is per-fectly natural and normal.

Only things go wrong. They always do. You pigeon-hole these people. You present them with their parts in your wholly civilised little play. And then they turn up slightly out of character and spoil everything.

Sandra, for instance, refuses to come as the downtrodden, lack-lustre little wife.

The problem is that the part doesn't suit her. For a start she isn't little. She is tall, taller than Ray, much taller than Helen.

She arrives at Ray's side a handsome shimmering Amazon, a long, full, silver-and-pink blouse falling in folds to her hips and plunging low at the front to show a rich and glorious cleavage.

Thick gold jewellery trickles triumphantly between the beautiful breasts and upon her arms and at her ears. She moves like an ancient queen who declines to be enslaved even in captivity.

And yet, with all this, it is her smile you notice first, an astonishing smile, stretching wide and unflagging across lips drawn bright and smooth and pink, vague and undirected and yet at the same time totally purposeful.

It is Helen's birthday.

Flanked by the loungers in the hall, Sandra, smiling, holds out a small gaudily packaged present.

She stoops from her very high heels to touch the side of Helen's face with the approximation of a kiss, a whisper-light affair, designed not to disturb the pink perfection of her lips or agitate her carefully assembled peace of mind.

As she draws back they stand for a moment facing each other, Sandra high upon her heels, a blaze of colour, throwing Helen into shadow and making her look, all of a sudden, not only small but really rather drab.

I remember Helen saying once, "Really, that woman gets herself done up like a Christmas tree," and she sniffed the sniff of one whose hips are slim and whose shoulders angular, one who knows the discreet charm of beige and grey and camel but one I think now, looking at the pair of them, who should not be asked to outface it here in her own hall with this razzle-dazzle of exotic beauty.

Yes, it is Sandra's smile and not her cleavage which draws people to her side at parties. Its beam, swinging like a searchlight across the room, stops people in their tracks, infusing them with a sense of obligation for the brilliant, unsolicited burst of light.

She sits now, perfectly at ease, one long leg hitched over the other, her skirt riding high over her knees, talking with a tired-looking young woman about the problem of her new and fractious baby girl.

She shakes her head in sympathy and sips her drink and smiles and in return she tells the woman of her own daughter, the daughter she bore for three months only, the daughter she went full of excitement to the office to tell Ray about, the daughter that afterwards she lost.

"I never knew, of course," she says quietly, with dignity, without undue emotion, "but I felt it was a girl."

The young woman has dark circles beneath her eyes. Before Sandra arrived she was ready to go home. Now she wants to stay. Something about Sandra, something in her eyes or her smile or her breasts says, Yes it's awful, but this is the way it is; really, we have only ourselves in the end; and in some way the woman is oddly satisfied.

She sends her husband for more wine. For herself and for Sandra.

Yes, it seems to me there is a truth about Sandra Ray has yet to tell Helen, a truth enshrined in the burnished gold of her skin, in the starburst of her hair and in the wide pink glory of her smile.

"Get your arms out of that water, Rose. I want to talk to you about business."

He doesn't, of course. He wants to talk to me about Helen.

"She's unhappy."

"Of course she's unhappy."

"I want you to look after her."

"She's a big girl. She can look after herself."

"I love her, you know that."

"Of course."

"But things are difficult at the moment."

"They would be."

"It's the boys. I can't leave the boys. Not yet anyway."

"Or Sandra."

"Oh Sandra."

• • •

I have never seen Ray drunk. He drinks steadily, reaching a plateau where he rests, never losing his coherence but becoming more carelessly and bitterly impatient with each succeeding drink. He's there now, I can see. His voice is sharply dismissive. He leans his head back against the wall.

"Sandra bores me."

"Yes?"

"You don't believe me?" His heavy-lidded eyes raise themselves a fraction in enquiry.

"I think it's only half the truth."

"She drives me crazy. But it's a strange thing, marriage."

He stares at the glass in his hand through the slits of his eyes, his voice shifting in embarrassment between the reverential and the mocking.

"Once, a long time ago, I went home unexpectedly. It was the middle of the day. She was lying on the sofa. Mark was asleep on her breast. Benjamin was beside her on the floor looking at a book. She stroked his head, even though she was asleep herself. I felt all choked inside. I don't know why. Crazy. The things you remember."

"I don't think you want to leave Sandra at all. You may love Helen but you don't want to marry her."

"It's not that simple."

"It never is."

"Anyway, I'm not sure I know what I want."

"But you do know what you don't want and you don't want Helen in the kitchen which is where women always end up when they move in with a man, no matter how much they try to guard against it. No, you want her where she is now, in the office next to you all day, making money for you."

"You're too smart for me, Rose, I've always said that."

"Nothing turns you on like a woman who's good at her job."

"Come back to us, Rose. I've just realised how much I miss you."

"And apart from anything else, you don't need another wife. You have a perfectly good one already."

"I'm amazed. I thought you'd be on Helen's side."

"I am, Ray. Believe me. I am."

"You don't approve of all this, do you, Rose?"
"I'm not sure I know what I approve of any longer."
"That's not like you, Rose."

"What am I going to do?"
"Probably what most men do in your circumstances."
"Which is?"
"Nothing. Absolutely nothing."

In the hall now there are kisses, ostentatious kisses, kisses for public consumption, "See how easy it all is" kisses. Kisses for Michael and Kathy who have just arrived.

"Michael, old man," says Ray, strolling leisurely up behind Helen, glass in hand.

Beside Michael, Kathy stands pretty and pale and still suffering from puppy fat, her hand trailing trustingly in his.

She says nothing, her eyes flicking constantly to his face, as if she is in a foreign country whose language she does not know and relies on him to do her speaking for her.

Andy was right. Kathy is "nice," nice and sweet and all those other things long since slipped out of fashion, words simple once to hand out as compliments, difficult now to grasp hold of.

Yes, Kathy is sweet and nice and very much in love with Michael. And who can blame Michael for falling in love in return with so much sweetness and niceness cast in his direction?

Wandering hand in hand they lock together in a doorway laughing. There Michael's eyes alight on Sandra. For a second, shame suffuses his face. Then he lays an arm about Kathy's waist and pulls her lightly and chastely to him, as if she were holy, as if she redeemed him in some way, as if her love in all its purity somehow atoned for the dreadful thing he did to Sandra.

"Rose, I *must* talk to you."

It is Jennifer, breathless with excitement on the landing at the top of the stairs.

"It's David. He's started something new."

Her cheeks are lightly flushed and her eyes sparkle with love.

"I must tell you about it. I can't keep it to myself. Really it's such a *brilliant* idea."

Her beautiful voice seems to take the word and hold it up to the light, to pour into it an ocean of admiration and devotion.

"It's a modular novel."

She utters the two last words in triumph, raising her head a fraction as she does so, her eyes glowing with pride.

"Each chapter, you see, Rose, is self-contained," she says, her hands turning elegantly in explanation in the air.

"Each can stand in its own right. It means they can be read in any order. The reader can move them around. Choose his or her own beginning and middle and ending. To all intents and purposes choose his or her own plot.

"You do know what this means, Rose?" she asks, a trace of impatience in her voice as she stares at me keenly in the silence that follows.

"Um...no, I don't think so. I don't think I do."

"It asks the most fundamental questions about the whole genre. It throws a vital area of responsibility over onto the reader. It's existentialist in the real sense of the word.

"It breathes new life into the novel, Rose."

I was walking down the stairs thinking, "David said that. I'll bet you David said that," when there was a crash at the front door and Martin all but fell in, a Martin very drunk and very boorish but very ashamed at the same time of the sound of a voice, which he knew to be his own, bellowing ahead of him at Jo as she crossed the hall, "Where you go, baby, I go."

"Baby," he said again, swaying in the hall, full of bravado and full of the fear of dying by the day of love for her, "where you go, I go."

He made an unsteady lunge trying to throw an arm around her shoulders, but she shrugged it off like an unwanted coat on a warm evening.

Now he stands in the middle of the room, wretched and isolated, turning his head slowly from side to side like a beast in pain as she forages at the food table among the wilting salads and hardening French bread.

"What happened?"

"He caught me as I was leaving the house. Rolled up in a

taxi and started bawling in the street. Woke up the kids next door. Had to bring him."

She snaps at the French bread and pâté, pulling it away contemptuously with her fine strong teeth.

"Every curtain was twitching in the street. God knows what I'm going to do with him. Out of his mind, of course."

Martin, being very drunk, needs someone to talk to. And if Jo will not oblige then he must find someone who will. By a stroke of frightful luck his eyes light on Kathy.

She sits in a low chair in the corner of the room, leaning her elbows upon her knees and gazing dreamily into the distance as she watches for Michael to return with her orange juice.

"Hallo, little girl," says Martin in his booming big bad wolf's voice, bowling joyously up to her and sitting down in the seat next to her belonging to Michael.

Yes, Martin is very drunk. He is also rather ashamed. But still he makes excuses to himself. He tells himself he is very unhappy and this air of tragedy, which he is thoroughly enjoying, makes his drunkenness appear the more foolish.

The drink has triggered the self-defence mechanism in his head, the device common to all that protects from hurt and humiliation by convincing the disappointed that losing the one that they love has not been the fault of everyday ennui, the unexciting reality of one person not loving another enough, but instead can be blamed upon the intervention of some external force of opposition, God, say, or Fate, or at least upon the genuinely tragic impossibility of one human loving two others at the same time.

"Could never have worked out," he is mumbling now to Kathy.

For Martin, the tragic hero, Kathy is not so much a person as a shape, a form, an essence, a ghostly confessor to whom he must tell everything. And so he does. He tells her everything.

He tells her how they made love that first time, the night Danny was born, how they had entered her house and thrown off their clothes. How they were mad for each other and had been for months. How they had taken no precautions.

How she had become pregnant.

He spews the words out in slurred bursts, his hand affectionately circling the back of Kathy's chair and drumming an occasional finger in emphasis upon her shoulder.

Poor Kathy.

Her secret smile is quite gone now and all her plump prettiness quite collapsed. Instead her face is an ugly study of shock and dismay, her cheeks, once apple red, as white as the frill around her neck.

In her lap her little puppy-fat fists clutch in prayer for the speedy return of Michael.

And yet when he does return he does not intervene to save her. To her dismay he does not remonstrate with Martin and put a stop to his unsavoury reminiscences.

No. He merely hands her the glass with an encouraging smile and then retreats to take up his post like a respectful courtier, silent but attentive at her shoulder.

She wants to turn to him, to throw him an agonised and pleading glance, but Martin's face almost touching hers makes it impossible, for the slightest swing of her head will bring her eyes into contact with his and worse, in the dirct line of fire of his fetid whisky-sodden breath.

And so she stares fixedly and horror-struck ahead, unable to see the expression of uncensorious delight on Michael's face as he tilts a fraction closer to catch the last of Martin's words as they hiss finally to a halt, weighed down with the whisky and the solemnity of what he has to say.

"Wants a divorce," he hears. "Knows all about it."

Poor Martin. Eyes blurred with mawkish tears, he still sees only Kathy.

He leans back, his eyes glazed and boring into her skirt where a last pinhead of his whisky spittle lies gleaming like a diamond.

And then he smiles uncertainly, looking at her, as if for the first time, in a friendly but unassuming fashion, as if not really sure who she is.

He draws his head back and blinks, trying to get her properly in focus. And then he shrugs, the smile quite empty, and raises his glass to her, draining off the last of his whisky.

"Wunnerful woman, Margaret," he says for no apparent reason and then collapses, falling flat across Kathy's lap, so that she recoils in disgust and then screams out loud, spilling her orange juice across her pale cotton skirt and across too the shoulder of Martin, as he rolls off her knees like a corpse to come to rest insensible upon the floor.

I helped Jo get Martin to the car, carrying him between us semi-conscious and mumbling.

As we dragged him along, his arms over our shoulders, his legs trailing, I told her what he had said and to whom he had said it.

She swore viciously under her breath and when we reached the car, manhandled him roughly into the back seat, where he fell immediately to snoring.

She would not let me go with her to the house.

"But how will you get him out of the car at the other end?" I asked.

"I won't," she said grimly, twisting the ignition key with an angry flick of her wrist. "He can sleep there."

And she rolled up the window, jammed her foot down hard upon the accelerator and roared off into the night.

Back inside now there is female duplicity in the kitchen. Jennifer and Helen, heads together as Helen slices more bread, enjoy the privacy of a wickedly womanly snigger.

In the lounge, the source of their amusement sits talking to David, legs rather too relaxed, skirt riding a little too high.

Sandra, shifting in her seat, crossing and re-crossing her legs with the effort she is making, attempts although quite drunk to make intelligent enquiry about his poetry.

Her glorious smile, which blazes still, receives from him in return a niggardly patronising upturn of the lips, bestowed upon her in short limp bursts, as he raises his head at the less intricate stages of assembling a roll-up.

Nearby, resting his shoulders against the wall, Ray surveys the pair of them over the rim of his glass, his swarthy face darker still with fury, his eyes two glittering slits of love and contempt for Sandra.

"Does it rhyme?" says Sandra.

"Does it pay?" snarls Ray.

The sound of Ray's fury makes David look up sharply from the half-finished cigarette. He adjusts his glasses, taking stock, adjusting too his smile from the condescending to the courteous.

"It doesn't rhyme," he says, looking from one to the other, "and it certainly doesn't pay."

"I wrote poetry when I was younger," says Sandra.

"Oh God," says Ray, clutching his glass to his chest and leaning his head back and back and back until his half-closed eyes roll up to the ceiling.

She shifts her body away from him, concentrating the whole of her attention tipsily on David.

"Of course," she says, "a lot of people write poetry when they're unhappy.

"As a matter of fact," she says, taking a large gulp of her drink and licking her lips noisily afterwards, "I've started writing poetry again."

There is an explosion of disgust from the wall as Ray heaves himself off and weaves to the door, the heavy links of his bracelet hitting his empty tumbler with a rich, hollow clink.

Sandra, affecting not to notice, launches on a monologue, her eyes opening and closing in sharp doll-like movements which slap the batwings of her lashes against the half-moons of coloured powder beneath her eyebrows.

She says, "Of course I only write for myself. I mean I wouldn't show it to anyone. But it means something to me. It helps me. I get something out of it. And that's all that counts really, isn't it?"

And so she goes on, prompted by engaging and insincere asides from David, until eventually she begins to bore him and he grows tired of playing the poet with her and he wishes she would go away and Jennifer would return in her place, Jennifer with her special smile, full of intellectual appreciation, delightfully fastidious, so different from Sandra's, beneath whose relentless and indiscriminating rays he is now beginning to shrivel and wither.

For Sandra has begun to repulse him. The proximity of her cleavage and her long sprawling legs disturb him. So does the replicated smile, imprinted in pink upon her glass, at which he stares with horrible fascination, trying to quell a feeling of rising panic.

His delicate soul shivers in horror at her awful vulgarity, so that a wan smile of relief escapes from his lips at

Jennifer pulling mocking faces in the doorway, before he manages to compose himself sufficiently to raise at her a witty and quizzical eyebrow.

Jennifer, smirking at him over Sandra's head, sits down upon the floor, noisily insisting she does not move.

She makes determined conversation, talking in the pointed and over-polite tone of one who would like it to be known that she makes an effort, an effort she would not normally be making were this not the party of a friend and were not this hopelessly unstimulating woman the wife of that friend's frightfully ill-married lover.

Then she, in turn, tires of Sandra and wishing her away, begins to intersperse her conversation with unkind little barbs *sotto voce* to David.

These Sandra does not understand. But cruelty communicates, and the smile, still wide and warm, eventually wavers and distorts a fraction with the pain, as the wicked pin-pricks of sound puncture her inebriation and her innate but wholly ineffectual innocence.

She rises to her feet and, broadening in farewell her impossible smile, sways to the door and out, to the sound of smothered laughter.

She walks towards the kitchen, tapping softly upon the parquet on her high silver sandals. There she pours another drink, slopping in the gin and then the tonic and throwing in some shrivelled ice from a bucket.

And then she turns to go. But too late.

For this party is a hostile place for Sandra.

Through the glass door connecting the kitchen so conveniently to the utility room, she can see Ray and Helen clamped together in a tight embrace.

Ray's mouth moves firmly upon Helen's. Their shoulders move in unison, their bodies burrowing closer and closer into each other in tiny, slow circles.

Naturally they are utterly absorbed. Naturally they do not see Sandra. But she sees them. And watches them. A voyeur.

She raises her glass to her lips and takes a long unhurried sip, still watching. And then she backs away slowly, sliding around the side of the doorway till they have slipped out of sight.

There she rests for a moment, leaning her head back and closing her eyes.

Her lips, no longer smiling, are slightly open in a long straight gash as if she has difficulty breathing.

Straightening up, she walks a few hesitant steps, placing her glass carefully upon the hall table. She taps quietly back into the darkened lounge, to the other end, away from David and Jennifer.

There she lowers herself, her skirt shooting up to her thighs as she begins scrabbling around the chair legs upon the floor.

"Can I help, Sandra?"

It is Michael, sitting with Kathy's hand tucked comfortingly in his.

She starts back in dismay at his voice, her face dead and white and frozen with unhappiness.

"Nothing," she says, her eyes on his. "Just my handbag."

Then, as she stares, her lips begin to twitch gently upwards at the corners, as if making the move of their own accord, as if aware of her agony and doing their best to pull her through it.

"Here," says Kathy, proud and pleased, holding out a bag, black and quilted and shiny and hanging from a long gaudy chain.

Sandra crosses the hall, firmly and with purpose, her bag swinging from her shoulder. She ascends the stairs with her rhythmic swaying walk and reaches the bathroom door which she pushes open and then closes behind her with a sharp snap of the bolt.

Inside she unzips the little bag and, pecking inside with her long pink finger-nails, lifts out a pouch whose contents she scatters with a clatter in the sink.

And then she stoops before the mirror, bending her body as if in some observance, doing what has always been done, doing, maybe, who knows, what always will be done by such as Sandra at times like these.

She smudges fresh colour beneath her brow, dusting it on cleverly and delicately with a tiny matted sponge. She lifts the wand of mascara and, pulling it from its tube with a soft plop, blackens and curls up her long doll-like lashes.

She takes a compact and snaps it open, taking from inside a brush with which she sweeps warm blushes of terracotta upon her ashy cheeks.

And finally, with a hand now quite firm and calm, she paints a new smile upon her drooping lips, a smile smooth and pink and totally purposeful again, an unflagging smile, a replacement smile, just like the old one which got lost somewhere, kicked carelessly under a chair perhaps or ground into the carpet, a fresh smile for all of us, for Ray and Helen, for Michael and Kathy, for Jennifer and David and for me, smiling back at the bottom of the stairs.

She awoke, you see, suddenly and saw him standing there. Or so he told me. And I believe him. For I think it's what she saw there then that gives her courage now.

What she saw was a nervous respectful little boy hanging back in the doorway.

She caught the momentary look of love and confusion upon his face, before it was lost and he became a man again. She caught it and filed it, in my submission. And has it still.

It's this, I think, that gives her heart, that makes her ask, a decade on, why she should give in.

It makes her ask why everything should be split up and spoilt just because Ray thinks himself in love with someone else.

A decade on it tells her all is far from lost. It tells her she can hold on, if she will but hold out. If she has the will to do so.

And who can doubt she has the will on the evidence of the luminous determination of that freshly painted smile?

11

I T began to seem like a honeymoon, the trip to Paris.

Twenty years ago, in an office dark green and grimy with the years, I beat out upon an old black upright type-writer a thousand such honeymoons. I beat them out on rounded keys that clacked and sometimes stuck. I beat out, at the *Weekly News*, brides who left with bridegrooms, newly wed, for Paris, in pillbox hats and suits with boxy jackets trimmed with fur, with shoes to tone and bag and gloves.

• • •

I told myself not to be foolish, and yet nonetheless I went shopping and bought expensive pyjamas, silky and pale, and satin underwear, setting myself up with a trousseau.

As I waited for him at the airport, I did my best to crush any feelings of romance, fearing them to be in some way inappropriate or perhaps even improper. But one thin silk strap refused to abide by the injunction. It slipped from my shoulder in shameless anticipation of the pleasure to come.

I watched him as he strode through the sliding doors, brogues clicking upon the marble, the battered brief-case swinging from one hand, a small well-used travel bag in the other.

"Rose. There you are."

"Paul. I'm sorry. Had my nose in this book. Didn't see you arrive."

In the bar we sat, unintimately, either side of a table, as a man and woman might sit and still be reckoned innocent if discovered there by friends.

"Extraordinary. Rose here is booked on the same flight as me."

I drank two bloody marys quickly and one more on the plane.

"Getting into the spirit of things?"

"It's not for pleasure. It's medicinal. I hate flying."

"After all the travelling you've done."

"It means nothing. It never gets any better."

"What exactly are you afraid of?"

"What the hell do you think I'm afraid of, hurtling along in this silly little cylinder thirty thousand feet up? Of crashing, of course, or getting blown up in the air or flying into another plane. Take your pick. Any one of those things scares the hell out of me."

"But it's illogical. Look at the statistics."

"I don't want to look at the statistics. For a start they don't include my plane."

"You're more likely to die in your car."

"Then I'll die in my car. Give me the choice and I'll die in my car. Happily. On the ground. Smashed against a tree or a wall or a lorry. Never mind. As long as it's not in the clouds, up here in this nowhere land above the earth. Dying, falling through the air, with nothing to clutch on to, watching the world rise up towards me in the last seconds of my life."

A forced note in both our voices made our lovers' banter slightly too emphatic. It came from fear. Fear of over-commitment, fear of inexperience, fear that here we were, suddenly alone together for two whole days and nights, with only a few brief hours in bed to go on.

"If God had meant us to fly," I said, leaning back in my seat and turning my head to him, "he'd have given us wings."

"But he did, Rose," he said. "We're up here, aren't we?"

It was dark when we landed at Paris, dark, with a chill wind and a fine drizzle. The taxi driver was a woman with a large Alsatian dog lying on the front seat, his nose on his paws towards us. He growled when Paul waved a hand in the air, pointing out a landmark. We laughed and so did the woman, and she and Paul began a conversation which I was unable to follow.

Her voice was low and husky and, even in a foreign language, conveyed laconical self-contentment. Her short dark hair gleamed in the headlights of other cars, and tiny diamond studs winked in her ears. In the mirror her eyes caught mine, dark, black-rimmed and amused.

"What were you talking about?" I asked to his back as the circular door catapulted it into the foyer.

"The dog," he said. "She says she is never afraid with the dog."

"She was attractive, wasn't she?" I said.

"Was she?" He wrinkled his brow. "I never noticed."

The room was on the ground floor, smelling a little of food, with a window barred and bolted against entry and a view through the city dirt of the backs of other hotels.

"If I was writing this as a novel," I said, "I'd have given us an attic room, with an open window and a view of tiled roofs gleaming in the early spring rain."

He took a bottle of wine from the duty-free carrier and a corkscrew from his travel bag, opening the bottle with a plop and returning from the bathroom with two tooth mugs into which he poured the wine.

"Never mind," he said, clinking his glass against mine. "Too cold to open the window anyway."

"And what are you going to do today, Rose?" he asked the next morning, his eyes twinkling at me over his French newspaper as though he were my guardian and I his ward of court.

"Just wander, I think. Frankly I'm not into museums and tourist trips and all that stuff."

"Quite right." His voice was warm with approval as he lifted his white bulbous coffee cup to his lips.

"I'm always telling people Paris isn't about the Louvre or the Eiffel Tower. It's a wonderful city for just wandering. Although, incidentally, it might be difficult to wander today. There's a demonstration on. According to the paper here..."

But something was worrying me. It had been lying there, at the back of my mind, nudging and winking and trying to attract my attention since he first suggested Paris. Now was not the time. But I thought perhaps... if it was carefully handled...

"Where was your mother from?"

"Lyon."

"So you haven't any relatives in Paris." I struggled to keep my voice neutral, but beneath the indifference it trembled with hope.

"Oh yes. As a matter of fact a favourite aunt. Jo and I used to stay here for half our summer holidays each year."

"Won't you call and see her?"

I did not look at him. Instead I reached for the butter and the conserve to demonstrate my lack of concern. In reply he lifted the coffee pot to pour more coffee he could not have wanted. But the pot was empty, and he turned in vain for a waiter.

"Well...no...I don't think so. There won't be time. It might be difficult."

"She might wonder why you weren't staying with her?"

"Well, not really. But I would feel I had to go to dinner at least."

"You could, you know. If you wanted to. I wouldn't go into a decline left on my own for a night."

"Now don't be silly. I didn't come to Paris to have dinner with my aunt."

Which is where I should have left it. When I could have touched his hand, kindling a charming little dalliance from the lingering sensuality, when I could have smiled warmly and magnanimously as if pleasantly defeated, when I could have let the whole thing go with "That's true."

But instead I said, "Your aunt must know Monica."

"She does, yes."

"She must have been at your wedding."

I tried to say it lightly but without success, as a dancer, injured or out of practise, attempts a delicate leap or turn, performing it shakily and without grace, making what should appear artless a grotesque demonstration of effort.

"Yes, she was."

"Monica must have wondered why you decided not to stay with her or at least make arrangements to go to see her."

He closed up his paper slowly and reluctantly, folding it upon the table with a small sigh of regret.

"It's no big deal, Rose. I just told her I had a lot of work to do. That I was using the opportunity to lock myself away and work on another chapter of the Conrad book."

"Does she know where you're staying?"

"Yes. I always tell her. In case of emergencies."

I wanted to gather my face together in a smile, to turn away to more coffee or rolls, but my eyes would not unfix themselves from his nor the one lonely question staring out of them refrain from forming itself on my silent half-open lips.

"She would never phone me," he said, answering it, adding a small shake of his head as if at the indelicate nature of the enquiry.

"The number is for emergencies, as I said. We both know that."

He lifted his paper from the table and pushed his chair back.

"She would never phone," he said again, more brusquely this time.

• • •

I knew he was right, of course. I knew she would never phone. It was part of their unspoken agreement, part of their arrangement in which I now too had a place.

Those who *think* their husband may be having an affair may one night, fortified by drink say, call his hotel to be sure. Those who know, for instance like Sandra, never do.

I imagined him walking to the conference, his tongue clicking in time to his shoes...the irritation...so unnecessary...really one simply didn't need it...perhaps it had not been a good idea...perhaps he should have stayed with his aunt after all.

I could not help feeling sorry for him. All he wanted, after all, was a pleasant weekend, with a little rest and relaxation between the academic skirmishing.

Kissing good-bye over the breakfast table, we joked to cover our disquiet.

I insisted on waving him off from the hotel steps in a farewell overblown with goodwill. I laughed a lot and played the fool. I danced around him and said, "Good luck with the paper," and then, "Be a star," and then went further and sang it, "Be a star, Be a star," an old trouper, of an age and from a time when unsuccessful heroines survived as clowns.

They called us "zany" then as I remember, or sometimes "kooky" with a "k."

Outside the hotel many of the shops were still shuttered and barred, and the streets were strangely empty as if the people had drained away.

I bought a paper from a news-stand hung about with magazines like flags. The newspaper seller was an old man with thin colourless hair and a wrinkled face and yellow watery eyes staring out from behind the collar of a too-large shabby greatcoat. Fiddling in my purse for money, I asked him in my poor French where the demonstration would pass.

But he shouted, "*Non, non,*" at me angrily and began berating me, snatching the coins from my hand and throwing them into an old tobacco tin where he jabbed at them with an angry finger as he scrabbled for change.

"He says, 'Don't go, you'll only encourage them.'"

I turned to face a young man cool and polite and very handsome.

"Tell him I'm sorry. Tell him I'm just a tourist."

The old man shrugged and grimaced as the young man spoke to him. He handed me my change, waving me away at the same time in disgust, his wrist in the air, which is when I saw the mark upon it, blurred and pale but still very shocking, which made me shiver and turn and hurry quickly away, for it was the first that I had seen and it left me feeling sick and inadequate and adrift in another world.

It was the music that reached me first, an opera chorus, stirring and familiar with new crude, patriotic words, sung by a rich, swelling contralto.

I tried to get away. But now it was too late, for every street I tried led only to the tide of thrusting banners.

They sang and chanted as they walked, on their faces the look of studious unconcern adopted by those unused to attention who know themselves, this once, to be watched.

And then suddenly the swaying stream hiccupped and jerked to a halt.

Four floors up on a building grey and peeling and shuttered, an old man stood upon a tiny iron-railed balcony. Despite his age, and he was very old, he stood ramrod straight, head in the air, as a huge tricolour passed beneath him.

His hair was grey and flattened to his head, his face ashy with age and entirely without expression. He wore an out-of-fashion wide-collared suit, pin-striped in musty moth-eaten black, with a row of bright medals and ribbons on his chest, the only patch of brightness as he stood, grey against the gun-metal building.

He might have been a statue but for a thick, short cigar which smoked lazily from one of the hands held stiffly at his sides. Below him the crowd grew larger as it slowed and stumbled to stare at him. And then some of them began to shout at him, "Come and join us," and, "We need you," and at their shouts he came to life.

In a sudden triumphant gesture he raised both arms wide in the air, lowering one hand to clamp the cigar firmly in his mouth before raising them again, higher and wider still, two fingers of each stiff in a grim, resolute "V" which he shook out at the crowd below, acknowledging their cheers and giving at the same time a hero's benediction.

In the marble-floored foyer the table marked "Information" was empty, but filtering through two massive oak doors left a little ajar was a voice which, despite the unfamiliar language, I recognised as his.

Inside, the room was long and old and very handsome with chandeliers and gold-framed paintings and glowering marble busts. The audience was grouped towards the front so that no one noticed me as I slipped quietly into a seat at the back.

He stood behind a lectern which he occasionally leant forward to grasp with both hands, his voice slowing and deepening with the movement. Otherwise he stood a foot or so back from it, one hand in his jacket pocket, the other darting forward occasionally to turn delicately the pages of his paper.

I could understand little of what he was saying. One word I recognised though, the French word, so much like the English, the word he uses so frequently when talking of Conrad, the word that slipped from his tongue in French with an even greater smoothness and finesse than it did in English, *"L'honneur, monsieur. Mais l'honneur."*

He looked handsome and impressive, and I could see that he was enjoying himself. He delights in conferences and conventions and owns up to it too, saving face by laughing at himself before others do it for him.

"I love it. The whole bit. The podium. The pomposity of it all. I freely admit it," he says, his eyes clear and unafraid and charmingly unashamed of his own boyish enthusiasm.

So many times, by the same method, does he turn the petty irritations of his personality into evidences of lovable eccentricity.

And that's how he looked. Eccentric. Impressive, yes, but in that faintly eccentric and wholly English fashion, his expensive, affectionately well-worn tweed jacket proclaiming parsimonious good taste, his shaggy hair shaming those with more time than he to attend to the barber before they arrived.

His great attraction, it occurred to me then as I watched him, is that he looks all the time as though he doesn't care, this man who lives his life with more assiduity than most.

I wanted more than anything to stay. But when I saw him step back from the lectern and take a deep breath, and lay a finger in quick contemplation upon his top lip and let out a long drawn-out *"donc"* as he prepared to conclude, I got up and slipped out.

Yes, I wanted to stay, and I was sad that I lacked the courage.

I wanted to walk to the front at the end, you see. I wanted to have him say, "Rose, how lovely."

I wanted him to put his hand lightly at my back and introduce me to his colleagues.

I wanted him to say, "This is Rose...a friend of mine," so that they would smile, quietly, behind their hands, these men of the world, these men of letters, so that they would say privately to themselves, "Of course. *Mais oui.* Such a good paper. Such a bright young man. One would expect it. To come to Paris. Without a woman. *Mon Dieu.* Unthinkable.

"L'honneur, monsieur. L'honneur."

You forget the most surprising things when a man you think you may love invites you to Paris. You forget important things, things that you should mention, things that have a bearing on the trip, that might complicate it or make it impractical, might even make it better, but which should at all events be discussed before you go.

For instance, I forgot that I was a vegetarian.

"Not even fish?"

"No. I thought you knew. It's why I always have the spaghetti napoli. Look, it's not a problem."

But it was. The waiter tapped his notebook on his thumb with disapproval. He was old and wore a frock coat and a long white apron and reminded me of the man on the balcony.

"You'll love the place," he had said. "Superb French cooking. And the waiters are magnificent. Ancient, some of them. Still wear the traditional dress."

"It's *perfectly* all right. I'll have an omelette. Actually I'd like an omelette. I mean it would be crazy to come to Paris and not have an omelette. Like going to New York and not having a hamburger."

"As a matter of fact I did."
"What?"
"Go to New York and not have a hamburger."
"You're very serious, Rose, over the serious things of life."
"You make it sound like a failing."
"No. Not at all. It's just... another way of living, that's all."
"My God, is that all? For a moment I was worried. Half the world living off the fat of the land while the other half starves. Droughts and dying babies. Fascism on the march again. Fancy me worrying my pretty little head about such things."
"That's not fair, Rose."
"To be frank, all this disgusts me."
It blows up out of nowhere, doesn't it? A squall. From a clear sky and a gently glittering sea. Suddenly there you are, twisting your napkin unhappily and taking sullen sips from the expensive unenjoyable wine.
"What, Rose? Good food, good wine? Just having a nice time?"
"It's so old-fashioned, apart from anything else. The days are gone when we should be treating food as an art form. That's why I'm a vegetarian. That's not so foolish, is it?"
"No. Not at all. I never meant to imply that."
His voice was earnest now and his face creased with the attractive world-weary lines.
"Rose. I do care. I care very much about these things. Look. My afternoon classes. I know it's not much. But it means more to me than all my other teaching. Helping them communicate their feelings seems to me to be more worthwhile than helping with the best Ph.D. thesis."
"Helping them to communicate what? That they're out of a job and haven't a hope in hell of getting one? That the best they can do is be grateful to you because you give up an hour of your tasteful, easy, well-paid life to shoot across to their tacky part of town to feel wonderfully humane at their expense?"

"The poor are always with us, Rose..."

"Oh spare me that. I mean imagine, the most shining example of the species and that was the best that he could come up with. Depressing, isn't it?"

"I was going to say, if you'd let me finish, that of course we have to do our best for the poor and the disadvantaged and ensure that they belong in society along with everyone else and not do what is being done at the moment which is deliberately exclude them to keep the better-off in the manner to which they've now become accustomed. But having accepted that, we're still entitled to our treats, Rose. I don't want this every night but neither do I want a life in which I am morally forbidden to have it at all. There are different martinets on different balconies, Rose."

"That's it, then, is it? The poor are always with us. Let's get on with our lives."

"That's got to be the most misunderstood line in history. It's a gentle joke, don't you see."

"No, frankly I don't see. I don't see at all."

"It's a gentle rueful joke. A joke about the way we are, which is part fine and part appalling, which produces a horrific system of inequalities but which can't just be wiped out at a stroke, Rose, precisely because it's based on what we are as human beings. It's a joke for Judas, don't you see. Judas the Militant, the perfectly proper socialist, who acknowledges only the grinding necessity of giving all of mankind a decent way of life and doesn't see that his plan is just too simple, that to carry it out he will have to eradicate something in the human spirit, and who doesn't understand that while life in black and white is cruel and unjust, uniform grey is not the answer."

"I go with Judas."

"We have to have a chance at the good things of life, Rose."

"While others haven't even a chance at the mediocre. We choose the size of our steak while they choose whether or not to make the effort to live for the next day's bowl of rice."

"You can't throw away everything, Rose, that isn't available to all. The truth is you'd have to throw away the things you really love. Books, art, music, they'd all have to go. Rewards, Rose. Treats that keep men aiming for the best. Mozart and Shakespeare weren't party hacks, Rose. Look, Judas and the rest of the disciples who moaned were all morally correct. It was proper that the alabaster box of ointment be sold and the money given to the poor. But Christ was right when he said that occasionally we have to turn our back on what is morally correct and with a rueful smile admit to being human, admit that there are things which give us enormous pleasure which don't belong to everyone and just occasionally we have to have them. It's not that we don't want to be morally perfect all the time. We can't be. We're human. There's a place for precious ointment, Rose."

"You're all theory, Paul. You've got a little pat solution to everything."

"No. You're the theorist, Rose. You're the one with the right and proper theory for solving the problems of mankind, which has one fundamental flaw, that it ignores the very basis of human nature itself. I'm the one who believes in the alabaster box, the rock on which all your theory founders.

"You're the theorist, Rose, not me. You're the Judas Iscariot."

And that's how it went on, through the asparagus starter and through my omelette and his steak, with me picking unhappily at the vegetables in heavy sauces and him waving away the waiter in irritation.

Eventually he put his two fingers to the bridge of his nose and screwed up his eyes and said, "Let's call a truce, Rose," and looked tired and burdened, as if something he had thought would be a pleasure had suddenly, for no apparent reason, turned into a trial.

In the taxi back to the hotel, the silence grew deeper and deeper. Back in the room he threw the key on the table beside the bed where it landed with a noisy, unfriendly clatter. He snapped on the spindle-legged television without speaking, and Bergman and Bogart appeared on the screen.

"Quelle chance," I said, smiling, but unable to keep an edge of sarcasm out of my voice.

He seemed to forget all about me then, as I lay beside him, watching, propped up upon the pillows, drinking wine from a tooth mug.

When he turned off the television at the end of the film, his face was blotchy with tears but he was quite himself again, charming and affectionate, as though the film and the tears had exorcised all his irritation.

He put his arm around me and kissed me, and I made fun of him, wiping away his tears.

"What's Hecuba to you?"

I was laughing at him, drunk and glad to be happy again. "What?"

"What's Hecuba to you. You know. In *Hamlet*. Where he's overcome with rage that the actor playing Aeneas can rant and rage and weep tears for Hecuba when Hamlet can do none of these things for his dead father."

"Ah yes.

'What's Hecuba to him, or he to her
That he should weep for her?'"

"Exactly.

'What would he do
Had he the motive and the cue for passion
That I have.'"

"You mean why do we weep for film characters? I don't know. It's an interesting question."

But I didn't mean it to be an interesting question. I didn't mean it to be a subject for debate. I didn't mean it to be something we could fence with skilfully and playfully and without pain. And because I was drunk by now I told him what I meant.

"I mean how come the New Man can weep for Rick and Ilsa but not, for instance, for Monica, for his wife Monica. Or for me."

And then it was too late.

He stared into his glass and then cleared his throat and swung his legs off the bed to walk to the window.

There he drew back the curtains and stared out at the box of space beyond, winking with lights.

His voice, when it came after what seemed like many minutes, strove to be friendly but was measured and precise and very chill.

"I wasn't aware you wanted to be wept for, Rose," he said.

Some time later I drained off the last of my wine and lay the glass with a quiet movement on the table beside the bed. I got noiselessly inside the covers, pulling them in misery over my face. And some time after that in the empty echoing silence I heard him return from the window and felt the bed give as he got in beside me, lying carefully and neatly so as not to touch me, like a husband returning late at night wishing to avoid an argument he knows will end in tears or sex.

And I turned and lay on my back and stared up at the ceiling at the faint pattern of light from the window and I thought, I know now why *Casablanca* makes grown men weep. I know now why they cry over it, peacefully and pleasurably, on Saturday nights, why they weep for Rick and Ilsa, who are nothing to them, with tears that are cheap and easy and undistressing.

They weep for innocence, for pure romance, for the loss of possibility. They weep for poor scripts and lousy endings and for the way life fails to compare with this perfect triangle of love, which never spoils and is never badly handled but which plays out forever for them, free of pain and free of faux pas and free of the danger of resolution.

Good-bye, Paris, I said to myself as the cloud hid the city from our sight. Not *au revoir*. Not till we meet again. No, a good old-fashioned British good-bye.

We tried to pretend the night before never happened. We wandered the quays hand in hand, but our hands were heavy and awkward as if not sure of the arrangement. We looked in closed shop windows and had coffees and drinks and sandwiches and made conversation which sputtered and lagged and fell into silence. Until eventually we surrendered and took refuge in a cinema where we watched an American film we could have seen any night at home.

And now as we banked sharply and swung away he said, "I'm sorry you didn't enjoy Paris, Rose."

"It's old," I said for no reason, "and cold."

"Yes, a pity about the weather," he said.

"It's nothing to do with the weather," I said, leaning my head back and closing my eyes and pretending to sleep.

The stewardess had a pretty French voice. She spoke across the intercom as if smiling at each one of us individually. She told us we would be landing soon and asked us politely to fasten our seat belts and put out our cigarettes.

"Nearly there," said Paul, looking up from his book, a resolutely friendly smile upon his face.

I was reaching over him and staring at the landing lights coming up to meet us when suddenly there was a lurch, and the plane, which had been dropping gently, lunged up again into the night.

The gentle hum of air-conditioned conversation disappeared in the scream of engines as we soared into the air, buffeted by crosswinds which sent long deep shudders along the fuselage.

An empty drinks trolley careered down the aisle, pursued by a stewardess, pale-faced and teetering on high heels, who caught it and dragged it back, twisting and turning as if it were alive, holding it awkwardly as she buckled herself back into her seat.

From beneath our feet there came a rumble and then a bang and then a long mechanical groan.

I turned my head to Paul, dumbly, in shame and pain and fear, forgetting the coolness and the silence between us.

"It's all right," he said. "It's all right. The wheels haven't come down, that's all. It's no big deal. It's happened to me before. It just means the pilot has to free them manually with a lever. That's the banging and rumbling you can hear. He'll just fly us around for a bit until they come down."

"And if they don't? If they don't come down?"

"Then they'll spray the runway with all that foam stuff and we'll bellyflop and we'll all have a wonderful time sliding down the chutes."

"I'm going to die."

I had never felt fear before like it, wet, cold fear, fear inside my eyes, beneath my armpits, between my legs, on my forehead, clinging to my hair, fear sickening and utterly shameless, fear that said there might be a God and if there was, Help me, Help me. No pacts. No promises. Only please, God, please.

"Nonsense." His voice was both stern and kind and he spoke as if to a child.

He reached into the duty-free bag and pulled out the cognac, ordering me to take a swig and then another, watching me, smiling and encouraging like a doctor.

They were deep gulps and they shot my head back and burnt my throat, but almost immediately there was a sense of pleasant confusion which blunted the fear.

"Now hold my hand tight and put your head on my shoulder and close your eyes tight shut."

"I don't want to die, Paul."

"We're not going to die."

"Don't let the plane crash, Paul."

"I wouldn't dream of it."

"I never saw anyone so scared," he said later, softly to my hair, his arms about me by the bed.

He was right. We flew around for twenty minutes or so till the wheels came down, then we landed perfectly safely. Still the baggage carousel was strangely silent with people standing in little knots talking quietly or exchanging grave grateful smiles with strangers.

"Don't go straight home, Paul," I said as we waited for my bag. "Don't go home," I said urgently, raising my voice.

He put his arm about me and shushed me softly, and now he whispers to my hair, tenderly but with amusement, "I never saw anyone so scared."

"If God had meant us to fly..." I said, smiling, not at all offended for once at his amusement, enjoying instead the glorious sensation of leaning upon the chest of a being so much wiser and calmer and braver than me.

Perhaps it was this that did it. This momentary return to uncritical admiration that tapped a gleaming seam of selflessness lying deep and undiscovered in the old abandoned mine shaft of the male spirit.

Yes, perhaps it was this, this simple acknowledged need to be weak for once, to be a lesser being, that released for once the rigid patterns and etiquettes of love-making, making each part of it complete in itself and no longer a stepping-stone or a staging-post or a prelude to an end, that left it aimless and open-ended and devoid of utility and, by definition therefore, truly erotic.

I broke a strap on the new silk undergarment as we threw off our clothes hurriedly upon the floor, to move towards the bed, arms about each other, a crab-like monstrosity.

His body felt freshly discovered beneath my finger-tips. I ran my hands down it and around it, astonished at its length and its breadth and the volume of space it needed upon the bed.

I stroked it lovingly, on the flatness of his stomach where it hollowed between the hip-bones like a boy's, along the firm thighs, across the pillar of his chest and down the arms that seemed so very long as they clasped themselves about me.

Lying flat upon him, I put my arms about his neck and covered his face with kisses, searching with each one for another longer and wider and deeper than the last, grinding myself into him as if to strangle him for love.

Taking him between my fingers very slowly, licking and sucking and burying my face in him, I lost for once the nebulous sense of discomfort which so often accompanies the ritual and which lies unexamined lest it be discovered to be revulsion.

Instead I was filled with a delighted sense of wonder at its graceless beauty, at its droll gravity, at the feel of its skin stretched taut and smooth, as if in supplication, as if petitioning to be touched.

I stroked it slowly as one strokes an artifact, finely carved, or a cloth of smoothest silk.

I cradled it and put my cheek against it and kissed it softly before submitting it, delicate and defenceless, to the rough advances of my tongue.

And in return my own body felt sharp and tight and wholly alive and full too of a monstrous need of him.

His fingers, both intrusive and adored, ran lightly over my body as if marking it out for the exercise of their own power and purpose. I turned my head away at the feel of them and at the delicious shame of his lips upon my breasts.

He drew back then to look at me, slowly, as if considering me and, eyes still upon my face, lowered his mouth drawn in lines of insolence to my ribs first and then further to the roundness of my belly.

He reached the mound of curling hair and did not stop but went on, below, beneath, his tongue searching, searching, as if somewhere in there was to be found the very heart of me and he would know where it was.

I heard the thin moan of pain in too much pleasure climbing upwards into the air. I clasped by knuckles and wrenched myself away a little from his grasp in the way of one who by turns desires and despairs, feeling themselves to be preyed upon by ecstasy.

And then it was all stop and do not stop leave me alone and do not go. It was all there and there and oh god not there and help me help me what is happening. It was all careful careful softly now gently gently almost there. It was faster faster almost there in a minute no not yet. It was all coming coming no not yet do not stop and faster now and faster faster faster now and coming coming rising up and higher now and there and there and here it is and coming coming yes oh yes oh yes oh yes oh god oh god oh god oh god.

And afterwards, eyes open wide upon the ceiling, there stole upon me the sickness that said, too much, too much too large a bite from this the too-sweet apple for which wrongdoing you will be cast out and wander empty old and cold and naked and forgetful of all the pleasure and utterly alone forever.

Which is when he threw himself upon me and hugged me and brought me in, banishing the sickness, rising some time later upon his knees to enter me, to slip easily into place and to finally come himself, gently and quietly like a prayer or a blessing or a whispered apology.

My heart is boiling over with love for him now, for his face upon the pillow next to mine, for the shape of his body beneath the blankets, for the sound of his breathing, for these things which here in this room, in this silence, belong now to me.

God forgive me, but I would rise early in the morning to black his boots. I would rise early, while it was still cold, long before the sun rose or the hooter went, to light the fire, to fry the bacon and slice the bread, thick and ungainly.

God forgive me, but I would wash the dust from his back,

sluice it down into the water, all of it into the water, to leave the back smooth and white and shining as it shines now in the silver light from the window.

For I don't care about Monica now.

No, I don't care if Monica sits, eyes vacant and miserable before the television, looking at her watch, chewing her lip, awaiting his return.

I don't care if she flicks from channel to channel in irritation, turning it off finally to pick up a book which several minutes later she tosses aside in disgust.

I don't care if she goes to the sideboard to pour a drink she doesn't want, if she spills it with a hand slightly shaking.

I don't care if she begins to walk up and down taking short angry jabs from a cigarette she has taken from a box and lit from a silver table lighter, a wedding present, long out of fashion, like all wedding presents, whose flame trembles with the vibration of her fingers.

I don't care if she puts a strained unhappy hand to push back her hair and if she stops in the action, catching a reflection of herself in the mirror, and stares at it for a long while, as if trying to recognise the face, as if searching in it for someone she knew a long time ago.

No, I don't care. Because I love him.

And I can't think of Monica now.

12

JENNIFER is not enjoying the opera.

She fidgets in the seat beside me.

She thinks the voices are weak and leans forward, craning her neck to hear. She thinks the orchestra is too loud and leans back again grimacing. She thinks she cannot see and so glares at the collar of the man in front who she thinks is taller than he should be.

She exclaimed with disgust as the offending slip of paper fell from her programme as we entered.

"What's the matter?"

"Oh I do think that's too bad. So annoying. When the tickets are so expensive. Really, if someone is indisposed, they should cancel the performance. No one wants to watch a stand-in. It's always so awful. You're on the edge of your seat the whole evening waiting for them to bump into someone or walk into the scenery."

Now adjusting her body for the umpteenth time, she leans over her elbow and hisses, "And I do so hate it sung in English."

Poor Jennifer. It is not the voices, or the orchestra, or her seat, or even the language which is spoiling her evening. The fact of the matter is that Jennifer bought two tickets for *Figaro*, one for herself and one for David, and were he here beside her now instead of me, the performance, notwithstanding any shortcomings, would almost certainly enchant her.

David caught Jennifer in the corridor outside his room this afternoon just as we were passing.

Jennifer's eyes were dropping demurely in deference to that which lay behind the door when suddenly it flew open and there he stood.

"Jennifer," he said, "I heard your voice." Which was unsurprising since, as always, she had laughed, a little overloudly, her pretty tinkling laugh just as we idled past his door-knob.

He looked, standing in the doorway, as if he was struggling to stay calm, in that way an agitated man will struggle to stay calm in the sustained belief that any unpleasantness can be avoided if only he will take the initiative and master his emotions, if only he will act with reason.

"I've been trying to get hold of you," he said.

The door clicked behind their disappearing voices as I walked on. Later she came to the library, appearing silently at my desk as I worked.

She bent her legs to lower herself so that her face was close to mine, whispering while looking away that David could not go to the opera and asking me if I would go instead.

"I can't," I said. "I have to work."

"Just one night. It'll do you good," she said, raising herself again as if the matter was settled.

When David said he couldn't go, Jennifer wanted to tear up the tickets. She wanted to rip them fiercely in two and

throw them into a bin somewhere, a horrible bin with cigarette ends and rotting fruit in it and flies buzzing all
around.

She wanted to go home and close the front door, speaking to no one.

She wanted to draw herself a bath and open a bottle of
her best wine, the sort she keeps now just for herself and
for David, and she wanted to sip it, her hair pinned up
and trailing perfectly in place in delicious dampened
whisps.

She wanted to lie in the bath and think of David, dream
of him, allow herself even a weep over him, a discreet
tasteful spatter of tears whose course she could follow in
the mirror tiles, tracking tasteful hairlines of mascara
down her pale unhappy cheeks.

She thought it possible, you see, that David might
change his mind, or rather something might change
it for him, a disagreement, say, between him and
Francie.

She thought it possible that he might yet come for her,
that he might let himself in with his key, quietly, late in
the evening, to ask her forgiveness and thus might suddenly appear before her, before her exquisitely wanton figure in the bath.

"David," she would say, staring at him wickedly through
her blood red crystal, "I didn't expect you. Have some
wine."

Yes, this is what she wanted. But then she became
frightened.

She said to herself, "Yes, but what if he doesn't come."
And as she said it, the vision of him appearing at the
bathroom door and sweeping her up into his arms, dripping and laughing, faded as if by magic at the words, and
she saw instead another of herself stumbling into bed
alone.

And then she saw that not going to the opera because
she could not go with David said too much about herself,
about her lack of purpose without him.

It told her too much about herself and made her worry,
further, about what it might also tell others. She knew she
must be more wily if she was to have him, to which end

she knew she must immediately disabuse him of any idea that her life waited upon his.

Which is why she is here at the opera, where she does not wish to be, merely so that she can say to David tomorrow, "Oh the opera...no problem...I went with Rose... you didn't miss much, as it happened..."

But now, in the bar in the interval, her good intentions are beginning to desert her. Her annoyance with me for not being David threatens to engulf her. She sits stiffly, looking about her without interest, one set of fingers tapping impatiently an arm of her chair.

I hate to be with Jennifer when she is like this. I have sat with her before in the cinema or over a meal, and have seen her fingers drum just like this, have felt the conversation drag as she strains against the dreadful disappointment of being in the company of women.

"I can't help it, Rose," she said once, in that curious way she has of being both deferential and defiant.

"I think it adds something if there's a man around. I just feel happier, that's all. I get on well with men. I like them."

And so here we are, an awkward threesome, Jennifer and I and the spectre of David on the spare seat between us.

"Really," she says, leaning forward to pick up her drink and breaking the silence, "The count doesn't even look the part. He's far too wimpish for an adulterer."

"You wouldn't know he was wimpish if you weren't obsessed with your opera glasses."

Jennifer has her own tiny mother-of-pearl opera glasses, bought from an antique shop at great expense and given to her, for her twenty-first birthday, by her opera-loving, fearfully devoted father. Which will give you some idea, I think, what Francie is up against.

"And the countess looks like a grandmother."

"Couldn't she be?"

"My goodness, no. Haven't you read the original Beaumarchais play? She's supposed to be a young wife, twenty-two or so, only a couple of years married when the count starts playing around."

"My God, that's terrible."

• • •

The countess is tall and elegant and wears her dark hair pinned high on her head. She reminds me for some reason of Monica.

She wanders the stage hiding behind a brave smile, clasping her dignity about her, giving way to tiny flutters of distraction. She raised her hands in prayer and then placed them flat to the sides of her head in misery and confusion as she sang her cavatina to the gods to beg for her philandering count.

"Love that once was mine restore me," she sang uncompromisingly in English, "Or in mercy let me die."

If I cared about Monica it might have broken my heart.

"My God, listen to what Beaumarchais says about her, 'She should display only a restrained tenderness and very moderate degree of resentment, above all nothing which might impair her amiable and virtuous character in the eyes of the audience.' What a bastard. Isn't that just like a man. Just a moderate degree of resentment, that's all she's allowed. Oh and worse, listen what he says about the count. He 'should be played with great dignity yet with grace and affability. The depravity of his morals should in no way detract from the elegance of his manners.' Can you believe that?"

But Jennifer's "mmm" is unappreciative and disinterested. I close the programme slowly with a sigh.

"You're right. It's not that good. Why don't we call it a day and go home?"

A bright gleam of hope shines out of the dreariness that has laid waste her eyes since we met. But the part she plays will not allow her to give in so quickly. She wants to spur the plan on but only with the illusion of her own indifference.

"I suppose it might improve," she says doubtfully, selecting her words carefully for their ambiguity and lack of conviction. "I suppose we ought to give it a little longer."

But as the bell for the end of the interval goes she does not move. Instead we watch together as the audience files back towards the auditorium, not looking at each other, until the last of them is gone and the performance can be heard resuming, when we settle back in our seats and smile at each other in relief and raise our glasses.

"I'm sorry about David," I say.

She waves a many-ringed hand in the air as if dismissing the subject. But I can see she wants to talk about him and that her struggle to remain silent is doomed to failure.

"Francie," she says finally, "is becoming a bloody nuisance."

"To tell you the truth," I say, clearing my throat, choosing my words now with care myself, "I've never understood about Francie. They are...?"

"Splitting up," she says defensively. "They're splitting up. He's leaving her."

"How long have they been together?"

"Oh, I don't know." Her voice is impatient, as at one perceived to be obsessed with the peripheral who should be concerning herself with the heart of the matter. "They were at school together."

"At school together?" My voice rises sharply in disbelief.

"Oh yes. Can you believe it? Childhood sweethearts. The whole bit."

"But...so...they must have been together for years. For as much as ten years perhaps."

With his granny glasses and his dope and his old canvas shoulder bag, David seems to belong to the sixties. And it's an illusion he makes no effort to dispel. But fate played a dreadful trick on David. He saw the sixties only as a boy becoming a teenager on the first day of the new decade. Which makes David twenty-six, six years younger than Jennifer.

"Still," she says, "it's not as if they're married."

"But that's immaterial, surely. I mean, if they've been together all those years."

"Not at all. Marriage is a commitment. One they were never prepared to make."

"'They' or 'he'?"

"It comes to the same thing in the end.

"Look," she says, "I do feel sorry for Francie."

But there is something deadly in Jennifer's tone. A patronising kindness which is merely a preliminary to a zealous bustling vigour with which, I can see, she will dispose of Francie.

"The fact is," she says briskly, "he doesn't love her anymore and she won't accept it. He's tried to sit down and talk to her but, like I've told you before, she won't listen. He just wants to move out, that's all."

And in with you, of course, Jennifer, and why not, I say to myself. Yes, why not? For what could Francie have to compare with a velvet sofa and a Victorian fireplace and a pot-planted backyard and a huge table overhung with a lamp and a big old brass bedstead and an astonishingly costly antique patchwork quilt?

"He'll leave her everything. He's said she can keep the furniture they bought. He doesn't want a thing. He just wants to go."

"So why couldn't David make it tonight?"

"Oh God." She clicks her tongue. "It was her birthday and he forgot. She'd bought all this stuff to cook him a meal. I mean on *her* birthday she cooks *him* a meal." Her voice rises in derision.

"Anyway she went crazy when he said he couldn't make it so he had to give in. And so there he is, presumably, sitting over her candle-lit dinner for two. Really, it's pathetic."

Her face has settled into deep unsympathetic scorn. It frightens me. I have to look away. I want to say to her, Don't say these things, Jennifer. Be the old Jennifer, the one I thought I knew, the one I liked to sit and watch, mild and tender-hearted before her fire, the flames playing upon the gold-brown loveliness of her hair.

"She must be very unhappy," I say, taking a wheedling tone in an attempt to persuade her to mercy.

"Look, she loves him. She's bound to be crazy at the thought of him going. She's bound to try and hold on to him. What would you do?"

Jennifer's face, though, shows only annoyance mixed with slight surprise. She does not want this show of sympathy for Francie. It is not the response she expects, the response to which she believes herself to be entitled. She suspects me of disloyalty. She feels betrayed. She wants to say, You're my friend, Rose. Why are you siding with Francie?

Instead she says stiffly, "Of course she's unhappy. But

then I'm unhappy." But she lies. She is far too confident of success to be unhappy. She is irritated, yes, because David is not here. But not unhappy. No. For she knows David will leave Francie. I see it in her eyes and her lips, pitiless and full of calm control, in the way she picks up her coat and sweeps her car keys, her gloves and her handbag off the table as if, at the same time, she sweeps away the last crumbs of Francie's hope upon the floor.

"The harsh fact is," says Jennifer, pulling on the gloves and speaking in the grave, faintly irascible voice of one faced with the task of putting another to rights, "that I love David and David loves me and that is something Francie will just have to accept."

"She probably just needs time," I say, crumbling before her severity.

"Time," says Jennifer sternly, "is something Francie has had plenty of."

She is on her feet now, looking down at me, her hands crossed before her, her handbag of hard dark leather hanging with military precision from her shoulder.

"Frankly," she says, "I can't understand her at all. Why doesn't she just let him go? The woman must have no pride at all."

Jennifer's bag is large and expensive, rounded at the bottom and fashioned like the bag of a soldier or a hunter, with a huge brass buckle to close it and little loops along the side, as if for bullets, where Jennifer puts her lipstick.

I used to think Jennifer all softness and gentleness, but I can see now that I was wrong. Faced with the task of getting what she wants, Jennifer is intractability incarnate.

I think now that Jennifer may be tougher than any of us. Tougher than me? Certainly. Tougher than Helen? Most likely. Tougher even than Jo? It's possible, yes, tougher even than Jo who, unpersuaded of Jennifer's ways, still calls her an idiot. How quaint. For there is nothing idiotic about Jennifer, nothing even mildly foolish or simple. Nothing of the ingenue. I suppose you might say love has brought out the best in Jennifer. It has isolated a certain determination in her, given her a certain clarity of purpose.

God, I feel sorry for Francie.

Getting up, I scrape my chair beneath the sternness of her gaze.

"Jennifer," I say thoughtfully, looking at her full in the face. "You don't think you're turning into a bit of a bitch, do you?"

The astonishing thing is that she never flinches. So totally in control is she and so completely confident that she remains utterly unaffronted.

"Really, Rose," she says calmly, with great sweetness, her eyes fixed on mine. "I don't know what's come over you lately. You're really quite changed. It must be something to do with Paul. I do hope there's nothing wrong between you."

And now I'll tell you something about adultery.

It's like a horse-race.

You're up among the front runners and you feel so good and you think nothing can stop you.

You look back over your shoulder and you see the others trailing and you think they can never catch up.

But you forget. That front runners can fall or just grow weary while those at the back can put on a spurt to surprise you, to show themselves as the ones with the staying power, so that you turn, suddenly, to find them beside you, taking the jumps that you falter before, and then in front of you with only their backs to your face and the finishing line up ahead.

I'll tell you, it's never a one-horse race, no matter how it looks at the time. There's nothing to say you won't be the one on the ground, your head against the rails, turning your face away from the drumming of the hooves as they pass you on the way to the winner's enclosure.

"Yes, there's something wrong between us," I say, smiling with reluctant admiration at Jennifer. "It's something really quite major. It's his wife. It's the fact that he's married. That's what's wrong between us."

13

I was worried for a while that I'd put too much of him in. That in recognising himself he'd be hurt. And I didn't want to hurt him. Even after everything. I didn't want to hurt him. But then I realised that in recognising himself, he wouldn't be hurt at all. In fact he'd be flattered. In this confused and ambiguous culture in which we live, to be painted self-admiring and self-centred is not to be insulted. "Gloriously arrogant" a fellow academic once called him for a paper he had written, and he was far from unflattered. And yet who would have thought "glorious" and "arrogant" could even fit coherently together, let alone be entwined as a compliment?

• • •

"Pick a book," he told us, Jennifer and me. "Pick something you're not studying. Something to read for fun. We'll do it in the tutorial next week."

He loves to do this. He announces it with the air of a conjurer pulling a rabbit from his hat. It makes him feel expansive and slightly unorthodox.

"I like to know what you're reading for pleasure," he says, the warm roguish twinkle making a welcome return to his eye.

And so I called his bluff and picked *Hollywood Wives*. I picked it because I remembered something he'd said to me when we were having a drink before one of his night classes.

"What I love about this sort of teaching is that it's so terrifically *unacademic*," he said, his eyes staring dreamily into the distance, his hands hanging loosely clasped between his knees.

"I mean these are not university students, Rose. These people are reading Jackie Collins, not Jane Austen, and if you want to make out a good case for Jane Austen, you've got to show she's at least as good a read as Ms. Collins."

And so he had to read *Hollywood Wives* and he read it faithfully from cover to cover, without enjoyment, and then talked about it dutifully, tossing leaden literary phrases around like lumps of dough.

"Almost Dickensian in its breadth," he said.

"And a bloody good read as well," I answered.

And so there will be one who will come after me, the buckle of whose book-bag I am not worthy to unloose. A woman wiser than me, less full of dreams, who will see things more clearly than I do.

"Pick a book," he will say to her, lounging on the sofa, as he hustles like a *hausfrau* in the corner.

"This one," she will say, so that he must turn, coffee jar and spoon still in hand, to face the bright, shiny cover she holds up to him over the head of her friend stretched out upon the rug.

"She was your student, wasn't she?" she will say, as they exchange amused glances behind his back bent again over the coffee mugs.

"Yes. I read the first draft of the novel actually, the first novel that is, the one she submitted for her finals."

"That must have been very exciting. Being the first person to read it?"

"It was, yes. Tremendously exciting."

But he speaks without enthusiasm. Formally. Like a man being cross-questioned in court. I see his knuckles, white and tight, as he grasps the brass rail of the witness box.

"Was it much different, that first version, from the one that eventually appeared?"

"Well, of course it was a first draft and she re-wrote it twice after that and filled it out considerably. The first version was much more ... economic."

"You sound as though you preferred it."

"No. Not necessarily. Although, as I said, it did have a certain economy of style, a certain crispness which I felt was lost in the final version."

"And of course the ending changed, too, didn't it?"

"Yes."

"How exactly did the first version end?"

Go on. Grope around you, son of a bitch. Reach for the cigarettes. Draw one from the packet and light it, slowly, reflectively. Blow a smoke ring into the air, and another, and smile at her as if contemplating the nuances of that first inadequate, inconclusive ending.

You, who never got past chapter four.

What do you give the man who has everything, a good job, a lovely home and a charming wife? You give him your heart and soul, that's what you give him. You give him your first novel, your dearest possession, your masterwork, your creation which, as you type the last line, you come to believe is dearer to you than life itself.

You lie in bed, full of his love-making, luxuriating in the romantic splendour of the gesture, dreaming of the moment when you will hand over to him You, between the hard black covers of the folder.

Oh you think you know me, touching my secret springs, seeing my abandonment, releasing to me your own in passionate but well-controlled draughts. But I have something here for you, something to carry you to my core. I have here Me, my soul, distilled into this my first novel, my first painful, self-indulgent, self-obsessed novel, my awk-ward, gawky, powerful tale of how I came to be what I am. Read it, Paul, and love me.

For that's why I'm giving it to you. Not for your sharp critical faculties. Not for you to comment on its construc-tion or the quality of its prose. But so that you will love me, Paul. So that you will take me in your arms and cover me with kisses and say, "Rose, my darling Rose. I never knew. Oh how I love you for what you have been through. But with me you will never be unhappy again..."

"I've got something for you. It's my novel. Well, the first draft anyway. I should like you to read it. To give me your opinion, I'm a bit unsure about the ending. It's hard for me to judge, you see, I'm too close to it now."

"I understand. Of course I'd be delighted to read it. I said that when I first heard about it."

"You'll be honest with me?"

"Of course."

"Don't misunderstand me. I'm not ashamed of it. I know some parts are over-written. But then when the blood's up and you're writing passionately, you can't stop at some good-taste line other people lay down for you. Look at Lawrence, exquisite prose one minute, slush and banality the next."

"I don't believe it. Is there a good word for Lawrence in there?"

"That's not fair. I've never denied the greatness of his prose... Obviously, you're the first person to read the novel."

"I'm flattered."

"There's no rush. I've plenty to be getting on with and I know you're busy."

"No. I know it's important to you and anyway I'm look-ing forward to it. This weekend..."

"Hi. Just thought I'd stick my head in. How are you?"

"Oh God, how am I? Absolutely frantic. How are you?"

"The same. Of course. Frantic. Absolutely frantic. Sud-denly the finals seem very close. I just wondered... if by any chance... but never mind... I'm sure you haven't had time... I can see you haven't... it's OK... don't worry."

"Oh Rose, I'm so sorry. I simply haven't had a minute. I picked it up half a dozen times. In fact I read the first chapter, which I think works enormously well. But I want to sit down to it calmly with plenty of time to spare, to really do it justice. By the way, it looks as though the Conrad programme is definitely going ahead."

"Oh fantastic. That's wonderful. You're going to be famous."

"I'm going down to see them tomorrow. I thought I'd take your novel with me to read on the train."

"Oh look, I'm sure you'll have lots of other things to think about..."

"No. Absolutely. I'm looking forward to it. I'll ring you when I get back."

Busk it, Paul, busk it. Play for time. You can do it. Give them the meditative gaze and the smoke ring and the smile, that wonderful warm academic man-of-the-people smile you do so well.

"Yes, I've read what she says about endings, but to be frank I think the whole thing is a bit over-stated. I don't remember the first ending being significantly different. A different emphasis, perhaps, a few minor changes in plot, but in essence I've always felt she was saying the same thing."

I took it back from him in the end, half-read. Brought it back home and closed the front door and dropped down onto the floor, hugging it, clutching it to me and swaying like an old woman whose child was lost and is found again.

"I'm sorry. I was reading it slowly. I didn't want to rush it. I was making notes."

"Who needs notes? It's a fucking novel. You're supposed to read it and enjoy it, not make notes."

"I'm sorry. I knew you wanted me to be honest. I wanted to be useful. I wanted to offer you constructive criticism."

"I don't want constructive criticism. Whoever said anything about constructive criticism? I want praise. Lots of it. I want you to tell me it's wonderful and, even better, that I'm wonderful to have written it."

"I'm sorry. You did say 'no rush.'"

"Of course I said 'no rush.' I said 'no rush' because it's the sort of polite meaningless thing you say when you hand your first novel to someone. You say 'no rush' when you mean, 'This is my life, take it and read it as soon as is humanly possible because I can't eat or think or sleep until I hear from you about whether it's good and I live, or whether it's crap and I die.'"

"I'm sorry…"

"So what's he like," they will say to her, this woman wiser than me, sitting on her carpet, before her fire, sitting over the coffee cups and the cheese and the French bread.

"I like him. He's a good tutor. Fancies himself, of course, but then which of them doesn't? Yes, I like him."

"So what do you think? Is he…?"

"'Paul'? Oh I don't know. It's funny listening to him talk about her. He's terribly uptight about it while all the time trying to appear frightfully relaxed and lofty and academic, blowing these ludicrous smoke rings in the air. Anyway, even if it's supposed to be him, it'll just be the old D. H. Lawrence and Jessie thing again, won't it?"

"Alternative versions of the same truth?"

"Absolutely. The old story. He did say one really interesting thing. He was talking, rather sadly, I thought. He said, 'You know some people have said writers are like cannibals. That they'd eat their young. But it's worse than that. There's no known name for what writers are. They'd chew off their own arm if they thought it would give them something to write about.'

"And then he went into this thing about Chekov, talking about how Trigorin was the best picture of a writer ever painted, walking around behind everyone, himself included, notebook in hand. And he said, 'She was a bit like that. Carried this huge brown canvas bag with her wherever she went. I asked her once, jokingly, what she had in it and she never smiled. She just said, "my notebooks," and sort of slipped the bag off her shoulder and cradled it in her arms.'"

"Is he married?"

"Oh yes. His wife comes in quite often. Nice woman. Bookish. Rather unglamorous. They have a little boy."

"You'll probably divorce Monica and marry your TV producer. That's what usually happens to a man who hits the big time at your time of life. Then Monica could marry whatsisname."

"He's married now with two children."

"When did that ever stop anyone?"

"You don't understand Monica. She's not like you. Underneath she's shy and very dependent."

"I don't believe I'm hearing this. Is this the beautiful Monica, high-powered owner of the bookshop with a lover in every genre?"

"One lover, one genre."

"One you know about."

"We've always been honest with each other."

"Oh yes, I forgot that."

"People aren't always what they appear on the surface, you know. Monica needs me in some way I can't explain. I think that's why she didn't go away with him."

"Guess what? I need you in some way I can't explain."

"You're playing games. You're not a bit alike. She simply couldn't cope on her own. She's very highly strung. She's an only child. Her parents died when she was young."

"Now there's a coincidence. I'm an only child and my parents died when I was young. And am I highly strung? I've got neuroses that you wouldn't believe. And as for being able to cope. Believe me it's all show. Behind this liberated, independent, self-possessed façade is a female teetering on the brink of confusion and collapse."

"You're not being honest. You know there's a world of difference between you and Monica. You've lived a different life."

"Luckily for you. You know what I think? I think your staying with Monica has nothing to do with Monica at all. I don't think you're staying for her, you're staying for yourself. You're not staying to boost Monica's confidence, you're staying to boost your own. Monica is like your launch pad. She provides you with a smooth take-off every time. She lights your blue-touched paper for you, and off you shoot into the great blue yonder to another affair knowing that you've always got Monica to come back to."

"I have to go."

"Monica services you like a car. She checks your ego before you travel and tops up your self-confidence and makes sure you're running smoothly for the woman you'll have an affair with while you're away."

"I'm sorry, I have to go."

"Of course you have to go. To a class for the unemployed, is it, or to hold the hand of a student who's having a nervous breakdown, or to do one of those other things which looks so noble and self-sacrificing from the outside but from the inside looking out is nothing but pure, sweet ego massage?"

"I'm sorry. I know you're still angry with me about the novel. I really wanted to finish it, believe me. I wish you'd give it back to me. I was impressed with what I read. Really, I was utterly absorbed."

"So absorbed you managed to take notes."

"We've been through all that."

"I wanted you to read it, goddamn it. I wanted you to sacrifice a little of your precious time to read it. To finish it. Was that so much to ask?"

"I'm sorry."

It seems to me, you see, not possible that you should love someone and not know that something is going wrong. This is the source of my guilt towards Monica. Towards Monica. And towards Margaret and Sandra and Francie too. For how could Margaret not have known about Jo before Martin blurted it out drunkenly one night? And what did Michael do on the phone but confirm Sandra's worst suspicions? And how could Francie have convinced herself it was artistic angst making David so distant and not another woman?

How is it possible, if you love someone, not to know it is all going wrong?

"Hi!"

"Oh, hi!"

"I just thought I'd ring to see how your diary looks."

"It looks black with a red edging..."

"Very funny."

"...and very full."

"What about a quick drink tonight?"

"Love to but I've got a rehearsal. The students have asked me to direct *The Seagull* for them."

"Before. We could go before."

"We're starting early. I have to audition."

"Tomorrow? I've found this place that does fresh pasta. I could make a meal."

"Sounds wonderful but I have an arts festival meeting. A few of us are grabbing a pizza together first so we can get our act together before meeting the council."

"Thursday?"

"Oh, Rose. I'm so sorry. I'm off to London again about the Conrad thing."

"And Friday night's a Monica night."

"Rose. I am sorry. You sound upset."

Yes, I'm upset. My lips and throat are tight with fighting the desire to whine down the phone to him, as women like me whine in good books when the best is past and the remaining chapters hold only the breaking up and the lesson learnt and the setting out again, alone, in stouter shoes.

I want to whine, "But Paul, I never see you." But I won't because I know this scene. Because I've read it in books and seen it in films. Because I know that, at the end of the line, his mouth will tighten and his brow furrow, only a little perhaps but enough to be detected, and he will begin talking to me in the low soothing voice he uses to calm distressed students, at the same time jamming the receiver beneath his chin to leave his hands free to re-arrange the papers on his desk and underline, with a witty exclamation, an elementary first-year spelling mistake.

"No. It's nothing. I'm a little tired, that's all."

"You're working too hard. Give yourself a break. Find a book you want to read for fun and enjoy yourself."

"I'll try another Jackie Collins."

They begin to drain away together. His interest and your confidence. The two things which finely intertwined make up the strand of the affair. You catch his eye for your self-confidence and self-sufficiency and independence of spirit whereupon he begins to chip and chew them all away by the simple means of not wanting you enough.

"I'll ring you next week."

The telephone begins to dominate your life. It grows, like something from Wonderland, out of all proportion to the rest of life, developing a personality of its own. It sits, idly, on the wall, its one huge stupid eye gazing sleepily at you across the room. And then, as if it has merely been biding its time to catch you unawares, it rings, screaming shrilly with laughter as you fly to lift the receiver.

"Oh Jennifer. It's you."

Your hand sweats with disappointment on the plastic. But the receiver is in your hand now. So why not ring him. Why not? He'll be pleased to hear from you. Probably he phoned when you were out at the shops. Probably he's wondering how you are. These are new times, after all. A woman may phone a man now without fear of dishonour.

Listen, says a small, dishonest voice in your ear, your problem is you haven't been direct enough with him. He doesn't know where he stands. After all, he thinks you're liberated, independent. It won't cross his mind that you're languishing at home waiting for him to call. It's not that he doesn't care. He's waiting for *you* to phone *him*. He's waiting for you to show him that you really care.

Listen, says the voice, you know he likes you. Remember what he whispered, trailing a hand down the line of your body, "Rose, you're so sensuous and you don't even know it." And what he said that night at the restaurant, at your favourite table in the corner, "I can talk to you, Rose," he said.

Talk to me. He said he could talk to me. Not to Monica. To me. Of course he didn't say he couldn't talk to Monica. But it was there, hiding in brackets afterwards, although of course we chose not to notice it because of this thing we have about thinking of Monica.

Phone him, says the voice, phone him now. He'll want to hear from you. It's no big deal. Just dial the number. Phone him now.

Oh God, I wish I'd never called him. Oh God, that was such a stupid thing to do. I should have waited till he called me. I feel sick, sick, sick.

If you've heard his voice full of excitement and enthusiasm and desire, if you've heard it say, "Rose, glad you called, I was about to call you," rushing down the line to you with its arms open wide, how it pierces you to hear it restrained and reserved and slightly defensive and holding out a cool, limp, unwelcoming hand.

"Rose, I'm so sorry. I've been so busy."

If you've heard your two voices running as one together like a leaping, gurgling stream splashing over the ends of each other's sentences, "I knew that you were going to say that," how the gaps and the silences hurt.

"Hello... are you still there?"

"Sorry, Rose. Forgive me. You caught me in the middle of some marking. I was trying to make sense of this essay."

He doesn't want to see me. There's someone else. I know it's that big handsome dark-haired one. The one that's always in his room. The star of the dramatic society. Of course. That's why he's directing. OK. He doesn't have to tell me to go. That's fine. I can be cool too. I can take it. So what? The things I've done. Places I've been. I'm not some shrinking violet. I'm not like Monica. It was fun. We went to bed together a few times. It was nice. Now it's over. Never mind. Oh God, I love him. Help me, Lord. Help me.

"Hell hath no fury..." she will say, smiling at her friends, the firelight playing on her hair.

"It's just revenge, isn't it, writing a novel about your unhappy love affair? I suppose that's why I feel sorry for him. He's really rather dignified about the whole thing, which I like. Frankly he's just pleasant and *nice*, for want of a better word. Good-looking in that dull academic way, but really quite ordinary."

"You see my main problem," she will say, wrinkling her brow, this woman oh oh oh so much wiser than me, "my main problem," she will say, "is thinking of him as 'Paul' at all."

14

HELEN spreads herself upon the sofa, pretending to be quite alone.

Her legs stretch out along the velvet, neatly crossed at the ankles. Beside her on the floor her high-heeled open-toed shoes stand smartly to attention, waiting to be called into service.

She turns the pages of a furniture catalogue, apparently engrossed in its pictures and its prices, occasionally lifting it closer when something of particular interest catches her eye.

Once she pours herself more wine, keeping her eyes half on the catalogue as she does so to ensure they do not catch mine. This makes her clumsy, and she strikes the glass with the bottle as she pours, sounding a small melodic ping.

In the kitchen Jennifer's food processor whirrs and screams.

I couldn't get Helen here myself, so I got Jennifer to do it for me.

"I don't understand. Why can't you ask her yourself?"

"It's a long story."

I sat on the sofa while she made the call on the phone on the wall in the hall. Behind my head I heard Helen answer and heard the silence after Jennifer asked her, "What are you doing on Thursday?" as she weighed up the dangers of committing herself.

In the end though she said "Nothing," a little reluctantly, and then "Great," without noticeable pleasure, when Jennifer said, "Good. Come to dinner. Just the three of us. You and me and Rose."

And now she lounges, trapped but trying to make the best of it, raising the glass newly poured to her lips.

I clear my throat, fiddling nervously with a dried grass bursting with a host of others from an antique jug in the empty fireplace.

"Helen," I say nervously, "what's twelve foot long and double glazed and will cost a fortune to replace?"

Michael phoned me, you see. He said he had to talk to me. He said he had to talk to me about Helen.

I said, "I'm busy, Michael. The exams are almost here. Can't you tell me on the phone?"

But he said, "No. I have to see you. It's important. I'll buy you lunch. You have to eat."

I met him in the same city centre wine bar where I bumped into him when he was miserable and out of work, but I could see from the door that he was a different man.

He hailed me from across the room with a large, loud gesture, simultaneously slapping someone else on the back in farewell, and then swaggering towards me all man of the world, the silver rings of a notebook protruding from his pocket.

"Lunch," he said jovially, shepherding me to a table in the corner. "I promised."

His eyes sparkled with drink and well-being. He went to the bar to buy wine, dazzling the barmaid with a smile and returning with the bottle dangling rakishly, along with the glasses, between his fingers.

He threw his cigarettes down on the table and took off his mac, whistling all the time very softly to himself, and then sat down, hoisting up his trousers at the knees with an air of complete satisfaction.

"You look well, Michael," I said.

But then the mood changed. He put a hand over his eyes and rubbed them, dragging it down over his face as if he were pulling away the mask of liveliness and jocularity. Beneath it the face was sombre and serious as if specially composed for the telling of grave news.

"I have to tell you," he said. "I think Helen's going crazy."

I leaned forward to protest, but he motioned me sharply to silence as the waitress laid down two plates of garish chilli and limp wet rice.

As soon as she moved away he raised a restraining hand.

"You'll understand," he said, "when I tell you what she did."

He cast a look sideways in each direction as if suspecting couples at neighbouring tables of attempting to listen and then leant in, over the plates, till his face almost touched mine.

His cheeks were flushed and shining from the wine and the heat. He clasped his hands together over his mouth, closing his eyes for a moment and taking a deep breath.

When eventually he spoke, he pronounced the words very slowly, as if to appreciate their seriousness, they must be understood separately as well as all together.

"She broke the picture window," he said.

Tiny drops of wine sprayed out into the air as I laughed, one little drop landing on a pudgy nicotined finger playing with the stem of his glass.

"My God, Michael. I thought it was going to be some-

thing serious. I thought she'd carved her initials on the
sacred turf of the green or something."

"Really, Rose," he said, his lips drawn tight with affront,
"I don't know why you have to make a joke of everything.
It is serious.

"It's twelve foot long and double glazed and it'll cost a
fortune to replace."

He'd taken Andy out. When they came back Andy went
next door, which was lucky because it meant he didn't see
what happened. It was only half past five, but there she
was, sitting on the sofa drinking. His voice rose a semi-
tone in disapproval. They'd been talking about the future.
It was all quite civilised. They were talking about Andy.
About how much they would get for the house, when suddenly she jumped off the sofa. Out of the blue. For no reason. Became completely hysterical. Started screaming at
him. Like a fishwife. And then picked up the empty
whisky glass and threw it deliberately, not accidentally
mind, no, deliberately, slap bang in the middle of the window.

"It was one of the best glasses, too," he said, a hurt expression on his face. "One of the ones the office gave us as
a wedding present."

And that wasn't the end of it. What did she do? Why, she
stood there laughing. *Laughing*. He'd tried to calm her
down. He'd actually tried slapping her.

"You did what?"

"You know like they do in films. But it didn't do any
good. Made her laugh even more, if you want to know the
truth."

"Perhaps you weren't masterful enough. Or perhaps
you're just not hero material, Michael."

And then she suddenly went quiet. Refused to talk to
him. Just sat with her head back on the chair. *Smiling*.
And that's how it had been ever since. She wouldn't talk to
him. At work they told him she was busy. At home Andy
was always there, or her mother, or else she was out. Now
she was dragging her feet on the divorce. Being difficult
about it. Not answering letters. And she'd promised to put

the house up for sale but nothing had happened.

"Talk to her for me, Rose," he said.

"Look, Rose," he said earnestly. "I'm not being unpleasant but these things have to be settled. We always promised whatever happened we'd have a civilised divorce. We'd agreed we'd make it easy with her admitting adultery. Now she won't make the statement that's needed. It's a simple matter. She doesn't even have to name Ray. And we'd agreed to put the house up for sale. But she's done nothing. We'll probably make about thirty thousand on it so there'll be enough for us both to put deposits down on other places even with her having a larger share. Look, I want Helen and Andy to have everything they need. Of course I do. And I'm willing to do everything for them. But I love Kathy. I want to marry her as soon as possible.

"I deserve to be happy, Rose," he said.

He picked up the fork and began to throw the rice and chilli furiously into his mouth, stirring it around and mixing it in together till it was a sloppy pink mess.

I left mine steaming untouched before me.

"Michael," I said, "what exactly was it you said to Helen just before she threw the glass?"

"We were talking about Ray," he said, raising innocent bloodshot eyes to mine. "I just told her Ray would never leave Sandra."

"Michael, you're something. Just when I think I have the measure of you, you go ahead and surprise me. The only question in my mind is why she didn't throw you through the picture window rather than the glass."

"I might have known you'd take her side. You women always stick together."

"If you might have known it, you might have saved us the trouble of having lunch together, particularly since you've ordered me a chilli when I'm a vegetarian."

I reached for my coat as I spoke, but he half rose, laying a hand on my arm in a placatory gesture.

"No, wait. I'm sorry. I'm sorry, Rose. Look, I'll get you something else. I'm just worried about her, if you want to know the truth. I think she may be on the edge of a nervous breakdown. For a start she's drinking far too much."

"Oh for God's sake, we're all drinking far too much. She's having an affair. It's part of the deal."

"Yes, but she has responsibilities. It's not good for Andy to see her drinking."

His voice blusters with pomposity and the pleasure of righteous anger.

"Really, Michael," I said coldly, pushing away the uneaten plate of chilli. "You can come over so sanctimonious sometimes. You seem to forget I've known you ten years. I've seen you falling-down drunk. I've seen you throw up over someone, and once you almost broke my arm in a drunken stupor pushing me against a filing cabinet in the approximation of an embrace. And unless you've given up your old habit of starting lunch at noon, you're half-pissed now. So let's cut out the 'Helen's drinking too much' bit, shall we."

"Christ, I'd forgotten all about that."

The bluster and the pomposity disappeared at a stroke to be replaced by a mildly lascivious smirk.

"What made you bring that up?"

"I thought it useful to remind you what a hypocritical asshole you are."

"All right. I accept I like a drink myself. But listen, you have to talk to her for me, Rose."

"What makes you think she'll listen to me?"

"You're her friend."

"Sorry to disappoint you, but Helen and I aren't exactly on speaking terms at the moment."

"Why not?"

"It's a long story and one I doubt that you would understand."

"Try me."

"She doesn't want to talk to me at the moment because she doesn't really approve of me having an affair."

"There you are," he said triumphantly, jabbing his fork in the air. "I told you she was crazy."

"Not at all. She's right."

"I give in. You're both crazy."

• • •

"All right, Michael," I said. "I will try to talk to Helen for you. I'll try and get her to see that she has to stop dragging her feet and get on with everything..."

"That's great, Rose. I knew I could depend on you."

"I haven't finished. In return you have to do something for me."

"Anything." He laid a foolish dramatic hand upon his heart.

"I want you to keep your mouth closed about Martin and Jo."

He furrowed his brow a second too late, like a third-rate actor with a poor sense of timing, jabbing his fork slowly into my discarded plate of chilli with all the care and concentration of a worker on an archaeological dig.

"What about Martin and Jo?" he asked eventually, dropping the fork and reaching for the cigarettes and looking up at me with a bright smile upon his face.

"Don't play games with me, Michael. I haven't the time. I was there. Scrabbling around on the floor collecting glasses. You were so intent on listening to Martin spill the beans you never even noticed me. He told you everything from Jo's abortion to her getting on the short list to Margaret wanting a divorce."

"Ah yes. I saw it in the papers. Her home seat. She has a good chance of getting nominated, I'd say. A good chance of winning, probably. Be a good story now with an election in the air if Margaret's kicking Martin out because of her."

"She isn't."

"We know that, do we?"

"Let's just say that we have good reason to believe that, left to settle on its own out of the limelight, the issue will fade away."

"A good story though, Rose. Our local MP philandering on the side."

"It's pathetic. What the hell does his private life matter? He's an MP, not a bloody bishop."

And now it was my turn to bluster. What I said went against what I thought and so I spoke sharply, angry at the situation and at the nature of the argument which had pushed me, with my own connivance, into the wrong corner of the ring.

"Doesn't matter to me a damn. But he's a public figure. He's expected to have better morals than the rest of us. That's the way it is. You know that."

"Don't tell me. You don't make the rules, you only follow them."

"Exactly."

The atmosphere between us now was ice cold as we traded amused and chilly smiles.

"You're a little old for this scoop stuff, aren't you, Michael?"

"Not really. As it happens it would suit me extremely well. There's a job going on the evening paper. If I could take a little story like this along to the interview, I think it would serve me rather well. In fact, to be frank, I think it might get me the job, which as you can imagine I shall need if I'm to be a married man again with a child from a previous marriage to support."

"Forget it, Michael, and I'll talk to Helen for you."

"Rose," he said, leaning back in his seat to stare at me, mocking but also curious through the wreaths of his cigarette smoke. "You amaze me. How can you be so naïve? So what if I promise not to say anything? What on earth makes you think I'd keep my promise? And anyway other people must know about Jo and Martin besides me."

"No. I don't think so. I think they've been surprisingly discreet. A few people in the party may know, but no one I think who would be interested in tipping anyone the wink. They're a loyal close-knit little band, the local party. No immediate grudge-bearers I can think of. There's Margaret, of course, but somehow I don't think she'd be keen to call in the papers."

I took the bottle and poured out the last of the wine, first into his glass and then into mine.

"It's a funny thing, adultery," I said.

I raised my glass, smiling at him in a friendly fashion over the rim.

"Remember Harry?" I said.

"Harry?"

"Queen's Award to Industry Harry."

"Oh, you mean Harry from Number Two."

"Yes, that Harry. Remember how we found him in the garage at the joint party?"

"I do indeed. At Number Four as I remember. With Gloria from Number Six." He chuckled, a fresh innocent chuckle, taking a long draw of his cigarette as he enjoyed the memory.

"That's right. Gloria from Number Six. How did we find them, Michael? That's to say, what were we doing at the time in the garage that we stumbled inadvertently across Harry and Gloria flat out upon the carpets?"

A curious queasy expression crossed the face that a moment before had been full of an open-hearted joyful hunger for gossip. He tried to calm it with another smirk but executed it so poorly that it sat lop-sided and uneasy-looking.

"Come on, Rose. After all these years. No sense in bringing that up now. It's all forgotten about long since."

"We went to the garage at Number Four, you and I, with the express intention of doing exactly what Harry and Gloria were doing, didn't we, Michael? But unfortunately they got there before us. Still, with a certain amount of ingenuity we managed it in the end, didn't we, Michael?"

"For God's sake, Rose. This is all so long ago."

I could see he wanted his irritation to sound commanding but instead it filtered away into the air limp and testy and nervous.

"It is, Michael, it is. A long time ago. How long? Let me think. It must be six or seven years. Before Andy was born anyway. A long time ago, yes. But not long enough ago, I think, not to enormously irritate Helen if she found out. Or worse perhaps. That's to say if Helen is dragging her feet about taking on the official role of adulterer in your marriage, it might encourage her reluctance further to discover she wasn't the first in the marriage to commit it. Might even lead her to question whether there were others. You were always rather popular with the women as I remember, Michael. There was a secretary, wasn't there, who used to rather push herself forward when you were around? Things might become very uncivilised then, might they not, Michael? Things might even become extremely mucky. Things might really drag on then, Michael. Who knows how long you might find yourself waiting before you are free to marry the lovely young Kathy? Particularly since Helen's in no hurry for a divorce because as you've always astutely pointed out, Ray will almost certainly never leave Sandra."

"You can't tell her. We both know that."

He smirked again through the cigarette smoke, a burst of returning bravado in his voice.

"You wouldn't dare. You couldn't tell your best friend you screwed her husband. That you screwed him at her party in the Wendy house in the garden of Number Seven."

He hooted raucously at the memory, rocking from side to side, his eyes fixed on mine full of bawdy scorn.

"To my eternal shame, Michael," I said quietly. "To my eternal shame."

"A very freeing thing, shame, Michael," I said. "It allows you to forgive yourself. Make no mistake that I will tell Helen. I will tell Helen, although it will undoubtedly blight our friendship which, as a matter of fact, I hold very dear. But I will do it if one breath of what Martin told you appears anywhere. Because if it does, Michael, I shall assume it came from you and no evidence to the contrary will convince me otherwise. I shall blame you, Michael, and I shall immediately tell Helen and shall further tell her how keen you were to turn the tacky little incident into a full-blooded affair. How, to use the quaint old-fashioned term, you pestered me. Yes, I shall tell Helen and she will unquestionably believe me."

I spoke calmly and quietly. Opposite me Michael sat silent, his face impassive, staring down into his glass.

"Bearing all this in mind, Michael, it seems to me to be very much in your interest to ensure that not one breath of Jo and Martin gets out. That is to say, should you hear anyone suggesting it to be the case that our local MP is philandering, as you so delicately put it, you will pour such professional scorn upon the story that no one will be in any doubt of its lack of substance. And they will believe you, Michael. You know why? Because you were a good reporter before you made the mistake of going into PR, to which, to be frank, you were totally unsuited, not being, in the main, a man of a diplomatic disposition. You were the best in the business, Michael. Probably will be that again. You'll get that job, Michael. Without this tawdry little piece of gossip to take with you. And I'll be pleased for you. I'm glad to see you back doing what you really want to do. And I'm glad about Kathy too. I'm glad you're going to be married. You're right. You deserve to be happy. She's a lovely girl. Young and lovely. Looking forward to getting married, I shouldn't wonder. Looking forward probably to having children. Young love, Michael. Doesn't like to wait, does it? And you wouldn't want to lose her. All that niceness and sweetness going to waste. All that love and admiration. I'd like to dance at your wedding, Michael. So let's keep it smooth, shall we? Let's have a nice, quick, good-tempered divorce. You know what? I think Helen will come round. I'm quite sure it's nothing. Just a word from a woman friend. That's all that's needed. I'll talk to her for you. I'm quite sure I can get her to see your point of view."

The long speech laid the dust of the conversation. Michael's lips stretched and contracted as he continued to stare into the glass, but no sound emerged from his mouth, and so the silence went on, oddly restful and satisfied, almost like the silence after making love.

He raised his head finally, taking a large drag of his cigarette as he looked at me, his face blank, flat and utterly unfriendly.

"Are you really ashamed that we made love?"

"Had sex, Michael. Let's get the terms right. Yes, I'm ashamed. Deeply. As I said."

"Why?"

"Because Helen is my friend and I love her dearly."

"Really. Is that all? How charmingly girlish."

"And for another reason too."

"Which is?"

"That you're a complete buffoon and you're utterly beneath me and it's bad enough that Helen married you but that I had sex with you as well is altogether too much."

"You bitch."

"Yes. Quite. How refreshing, Michael, that after all these years we at last understand each other."

"Well," he said triumphantly, a sneer slanting his lips in a jagged line across his face, "you might be ashamed of our little liaison, but I see it hasn't put you off married men altogether."

Beneath the wavy, rakishly old-fashioned hair that falls across his forehead, the tiny beads of perspiration have become large drops of sweat. As if aware of my eyes, he picked up a paper napkin and wiped them away defensively. In the space between the edges of his jacket, a striped blue and white shirt strained at the buttons across his chest.

"Michael," I said, "best to let hostilities cease."

"Who is he anyway? Anyone I know?"

"No. No one you know."

"Going to leave his wife, is he?"

"No, I think not."

"Oh dear me. Just carrying on, is he? Rose has got her comeuppance at last, has she?"

"What for, Michael? For not wanting you?"

"You could have done worse."

As he said it, he shrugged and smiled, trying to pretend it was a joke. But I could see it wasn't. That he was telling himself something he wanted to be true.

And so I smiled too, smiled an unhappy smile, smiled at the vulnerability poking through the threadbare self-image, smiled at him in the awkward affected way you smile at the comic coat of a tramp, ignoring with determination the dirt and the disease underneath and the stench of neglect that catches in the nostrils as he passes.

"I don't think so, Michael," I said, shaking my head. "Frankly I don't think so. Not from what I remember of what went on in the Wendy house."

"I'll give you a clue, Helen," I say to the figure still staring with studied determination at the catalogue.

"Michael says it was one of the best glasses. One of the ones the office gave you for a wedding present."

And now she looks up slowly as if the words have taken a long time to penetrate. She stares at the window, pursing her lips and then finally closes the catalogue deliberately and without haste, turning her head majestically towards me.

"He called me," I say, speaking quickly and smiling a nervous, mild-mannered, mollifying smile. "He said he had to talk to me. We had lunch. He told me what happened. I told him he was lucky you didn't throw him through the picture window."

At first she ignores my efforts at appeasement, looking at me coldly and without expression. But then suddenly she smiles herself, a bright friendly smile that spreads all over her face.

She tosses the catalogue aside, lifting the glass to her lips.

"You cannot imagine," she says, her face suddenly animated with the delight of shared enthusiasm, "the sheer damn exhilaration of smashing that bloody picture window."

"It was wonderful," she says. "I can't tell you how good it felt. Suddenly all the worry and the hurt and tension seemed to melt away.

"The glass seemed to fly through the air in slow motion," she says, her hands weaving an elegant arc above her head. "It hit right in the middle with this wonderful hard crack, and all the inside came crashing out and all the outside spider-webbed."

She might have been a scientist describing a successful experiment.

"And then suddenly," she says, "I couldn't see that damn green anymore or those pathetic little trees."

"And one of the best glasses, too."

"Waterford glass," she says with satisfaction. "Waterford glass."

"The problem is, Rose, Michael's become so nauseatingly big brotherly since he fell in love."

"It's a male trait. I've noticed it before. Falling in love makes them feel so wonderfully humane."

"Every time he comes round to see Andy he uses it as an excuse to tell me what I'm doing wrong in my life."

"Not to mention turning them instantly into fully qualified and experienced therapists."

"He thinks I'm drinking too much because I'm always drinking when he arrives. I'm always drinking when he arrives because it's the only way I can face another session of him telling me I'm drinking too much."

"Ex-husbands are always very hot on alcohol abuse in wives."

"Anyway he'd just got onto his favourite theme, that Ray would never leave Sandra. His voice was droning on and on. I looked up and all I could see were these lips moving, saying Ray this and Ray that. Probably I was drunk but anyway that was it. I just picked up the glass and threw it. Anything to make him shut up, I thought. And then as soon as I'd done it, I felt so good, I started to laugh and I couldn't stop. He put on my apron and did his housewife bit with the dustpan and brush, and that made me laugh even more. And then he thought I was hysterical and tried to hit me, you know, like they do in films. Masterfully. But he couldn't do it. He was nervous and came at me the wrong way and the slap kept slipping off the side of my face. He tried again and again and the slaps got quite hard, but the more he slapped the more I laughed, he looked so funny, slapping me with my frilly apron on.

"In the end I said to him, 'Stop it, Michael. For God's sake, stop it. Don't hit me again. I'll die laughing if you do. Honest to God you'll kill me if you go on.'"

We are laughing now, both of us, rocking backwards and forward and kicking our legs in the air like children.

The noise brings Jennifer in from the kitchen.

I tell her, "Helen broke the picture window," which sets us off again, howling, until we are finally hushed by the sight of Jennifer before us, like a doting parent, her face and dripping rubber gloves a picture of friendly puzzlement.

We try to tell her what happened, but still she only smiles gently, politely, so that we stop laughing and insist on filling her glass and toasting her as the cook and then get up and go with her to the kitchen, to help her make the salad and lay the table and do all the other things she would rather do herself, to close up the silence between us and smooth over the bafflement.

Laying out the silverware beneath the handsome hanging lamp I say, "He wanted me to talk to you. He said you were dragging your feet over the divorce and selling the house."

"It's the strangest thing," she says, staring thoughtfully at a napkin as she rolls it into a ring.

"I have to make this statement. A confession statement, they call it," she says, pulling a wry face. "Confession. Because you've done something wrong. Oh, I know it's nothing really. Just admitting I committed adultery. Just times and places. I don't even have to mention accounts."

She looks up and giggles, but then the laughter falls away and her face is sad.

"I don't even have to mention his name," she says.

For a moment there is silence, then she seems to mentally shake herself, becoming brisk.

"It's just a formality. I know that. We agreed. It'll give us a quick divorce. But for some reason I can't face doing it. It's crazy. I don't know why. It's so illogical. But I think I just don't want to see it down in print that I'm having an affair. As if there's something...oh I don't know... unpleasant about it, something..."

"Dishonourable?"

"No. Not at all, damn you," she says smiling.

"Nothing to worry about then, I'd say," I say, smiling back. "Best to get it done then. Best to get it over with."

"First thing tomorrow morning," she says. "As a matter of fact it won't take me long. The solicitor told me just a few times and places as though I had plenty to choose from. As a matter of fact the sum total of the few I've got would look pretty silly sitting in the middle of a sheet of foolscap paper."

"Don't worry. Your honour will be saved. They'll assume they're just specimen charges."

"The times you've made love," she says, "they're embarrassingly few when you count them up, aren't they?"

"So few you can't believe you built a love affair around them."

"You too?" she says.

"He doesn't love me," I say flatly and miserably. "It's not surprising. It's not at all surprising. The only thing that's surprising is that I'm surprised."

"I understand," she says. "You look at what you are, don't you, what he is and what you are. You look at all the evidence, or what you think is the evidence, at the way things are and the way you think they could be and it seems only logical that he should love you."

"It's true. And now I'm shocked to the core that he doesn't love me because although I didn't realise it, I'd presumed that he would. And now I'm living in this strange new world where everything is jagged and badly fitting. And I have this odd new pain below my ribs that wasn't there before that comes from straining all the time against the hurt. And I see now that it never occurred to him to love me. He never thought of it as a love situation. He thought we were both just in it for a good time. Love was never on the agenda."

From the kitchen comes the violent shriek of grinding coffee beans.

"Answer me this," I say, "is there something wrong with us? Are we out of step? Should we be able to handle an affair? Is it something we're supposed to be able to do like once we were supposed to arrange flowers and cook coq au vin?"

"I don't know, Rose."

"Answer me this, what is it that they want?"

"Ah, if we only knew that," she says, smiling a little sadly. "If we only knew that."

15

Jo is giving a dinner party.

"I thought a goulash."

We always have goulash at Jo's. Goulash, fierce and tasteless, with baked potatoes, old and full of eyes, and a large uninviting bowl of workaday salad.

"With just baked potatoes and salad, I thought, and melon to start."

We always have melon to start and to finish a rather dull cheeseboard, Cheddar and Stilton and squashed and over-ripe Brie.

"And just cheese and biscuits."

• • •

Jo loathes cooking, you see.

She gives dinner parties only when no other means can be found of assembling around a table the people she requires for one of her schemes.

Like Marcus.

"Marcus!"

"Yes, I bumped into him the other day in the street. It was so nice to see him again. I thought I'd invite him round."

I've never heard her use the word "nice" before in connection with a man. It sounds awkward in her mouth, puerile, like unaccustomed baby talk from a childless adult.

And Terry and Dorothea.

"Who?"

"Secretary of the local party back home and his wife. They're up here visiting his parents. I thought it would be friendly to ask them too."

I can't remember her being concerned with being "friendly" before. The word shrivels with lack of conviction at the other end of the phone.

"And Martin and Margaret," she finishes, casually triumphant.

I understand. What we have here is a charade for this Terry and Dorothea, a pageant, a peep-show, a little armchair theatre.

"I'm busy. The exams start in a couple of weeks. I want to be excused."

"Nonsense. You can't work all the time. Ask your tutor."

"I'd like to, but as it happens I haven't seen him."

"I warned you, Rose, I warned you," she says with the sigh of one who is seldom listened to. "Come early for a drink."

What she meant, of course, was come early and do the salad. Chopping the peppers now with a blunt and highly unsuitable knife, I ponder the artfulness of women.

"So Margaret and Martin have patched it up?"

"Of course."

"It's nice of her, I must say, to come round here to bolster your image. To lay for you any ugly rumours that might perchance have reached the ears of your future constituency secretary."

"Why not? She's as keen as I am to show the marriage is back on its feet."

"Didn't you feel embarrassed at least inviting her? I mean, talking to her on the phone?"

"I've spoken to her hundreds of times when I've needed to leave messages for Martin."

"Strange, isn't it? In books they always put the phone down when they hear the wife's voice."

"In books, in books," she says impatiently, stirring the pan of steaming goulash. "That's your trouble, Rose. It's always in books. Look, for four years we've played the game of pretending the affair wasn't going on. Now we're pretending it never happened. She doesn't want to throw it in my face. I don't want to throw it in hers. That's the way women do it."

"I don't understand. How can she come to dinner with the woman who's been having an affair with her husband for the past four years?"

"Why not? What's there to be embarrassed or ashamed about? I've used him for my purposes, she's used him for hers. I've used him for a lover. She's used him as a husband and father."

"Not much of a husband."

"Look, I don't need this moralistic shit from you."

She faces me across the old gas stove, her eyes and lips crackling with anger, a ladle still in her hand. Old grime and grease run in long trickles down the door and sides of the oven, and on the top, beneath the pan, the jet burns feebly through encrusted spills.

"If you want to feel awful about Monica that's fine, but don't expect me to feel the same way about Margaret, because I don't. Martin was always going to have an affair with the male menopause threatening. Luckily he had it with someone who didn't want him to leave his wife and kids. Pity my brother's not so lucky."

"What's that supposed to mean?"

"Oh for God's sake, you're eating your heart out for him. You're desperate for him to leave Monica. You can't wait to

start scouring the house ads for some little terraced
number where you can start stripping the floorboards together and putting up the Laura Ashley wallpaper. You
want the whole bit, don't you, Rose. Which doesn't matter
but I just wish you'd admit it, that's all, and get on with
your own life and leave me to get on with mine."

She swept up an armful of cutlery, napkins and table-
cloth, and stalked out as she spoke, and now her disembod-
ied voice floats through the white Artexed doorway from
the dining room along the passage.

"I've told you before, Rose," she shouts. "You make
things too complicated. Too dramatic. You think everyone
thinks the way you do. You think you understand all
women on the grounds that you're a woman yourself. But
that's a big mistake. Women are an infinitely varied sex,
Rose. There's no reason why you should understand us all."

Jo's house is extraordinary. She bought it a decade ago
from a sixties survivor who was selling up lock, stock and
barrel to move to a croft in the Orkneys.

Uneasy with doors, he had them removed, shaping the
doorways into arches. Unable to countenance wallpaper,
he plastered Artex everywhere, so that wandering around
the warren of white-washed rooms now reminds you of
nothing so much as being back in one of those little Spanish bars you stumbled on during your first time abroad,
tucked away in the foothills, where you thought the guitars weren't played for the tourists and where you drank
cheap red wine and read Hemingway by candle-light and
wrote postcards to people still taking holidays at home.

You see, Jo changed nothing when she moved in. She
even left his posters up, which is why Che Guevara
watches me now from the kitchen wall, watches me with
the beginnings of a smile as inscrutable as the Mona
Lisa's, a faint smile which by some old magic transforms
itself into a revolutionary sneer for the young guard who
stand before it with ill-disguised reverence, much impressed with the political soundness of the owner of the
house as exampled by the face of this saint staring out,
forever young and beautiful, from the fading, greying
Artex.

• • •

But now the house, like all of us, shows the signs of slipping quietly with sixties gentility into early middle age.

It is beginning to crumble and crack and badly needs re-decorating.

"The guttering's gone," says Marcus cheerfully, craning his head back at the front door.

"And the roof's leaking again. Hallo, Marcus."

"Hallo, Rose."

Once Jo would have been furious if Marcus was early. Now to my surprise she appears pleased. She takes him by the arm and leads him effusively to a chair.

"Whatever you do," she used to say, "don't start Marcus on his bloody polls."

Now she hands him a glass with a dazzling smile and says, "So what's the latest from the great British public, Marcus?"

Marcus works in market research. There's a coolness about him that frightens me. I wonder, if he were called upon to do so, whether he might not collate the statistics of atrocities with the merest pucker of disquiet between his eyebrows. For, you see, it's percentages that concern Marcus, not people. He's not interested in what we do. Only in how many of us do it.

Marcus is sandy-haired and pale and looks as though he has been kept from the light. He is thin and not over-tall, and polio as a child has left him with a small stoop to his shoulders so that from the side he looks like one of his own eternally recurring question marks.

There's something innocent about him, something worryingly unworldly, something monastic about him, locked away in his pollster's cell all day.

It's hard to imagine Marcus in love. And yet he fell in love with Jo.

It was just after the election. She had worked very hard and had grown tired and, despite all her protestation about love, I think she was in some confusion over Martin.

He took her out for expensive meals and away for weekends in the country, which gave her time to think and rest and at the same time usefully unsettled Martin.

But more than that he began to organise her life. He fixed things around the house, like the roof which was letting in rain on the battered but beautiful hexagonal table she bought with the house.

He cut back the bushes in the front garden so that she could walk up the path again, put up the shelves that she needed and mended the kettle.

He changed the plugs and the battery in the car so that it started in the mornings. He waited in for the coalman and checked the bill and found she was being overcharged. He cooked her meals and ran a bath when she came home tired and, because he loathes all forms of grubbiness, even spring-cleaned the house.

"He's better than a wife," she said once, smirking and admiring herself in the toes of her freshly polished boots.

And for a while she liked it. She liked someone looking after her. She enjoyed closing her eyes and putting her head back and listening to someone else get on with the business of living for her.

But then she began to gain her strength again and as she did so, he grew irksome to her.

And at the same time she found she was pregnant by Martin.

Poor Marcus. Only he could be unlucky enough to ask Jo to marry him on the day she found she was pregnant.

I remember his pale lashes blinking in astonishment over his light blue eyes as her voice lashed him in the face the night he declared himself.

He had slipped his proposal through her letter-box and had gone to the pub to work up the courage to receive her answer.

The proposal was doubly important to Marcus. In the first place he had never asked a woman to marry him before, but more importantly, he had never either made a deliberate attempt to be funny.

Marcus, you see, has no sense of humour. Not that he is dour or humourless. It's simply that humour doesn't figure in his life. He's entirely liberated about it. He's happy for other people to laugh and play japes. It's just that it's something he doesn't do himself. Make a joke before Marcus and he will dutifully force a smile while his brow wrinkles in genial puzzlement.

And so a great deal of serious thought had gone into the witty presentation of his marriage proposal.

He had worded it like one of his surveys, with questions like, "Do you believe marriage between two like-minded mature people can work?" with little boxes for "yes" and "no" and "don't know."

The last question was "Will you marry me?"

She found it lying on the mat when she returned with me from the doctor's, and Marcus burst in a few minutes later.

Her voice cracked the air like a whip.

"Not only do I not love you, Marcus," she said, "but it so happens I have just discovered I am pregnant by someone else. No, don't go, Rose," she bellowed in irritation as she caught me trying to creep down the passage. "Marcus is just leaving."

I felt so sorry for him, a thin, hunched, bemused little question mark, slipping slowly out through the front door and down his own freshly cleared front path.

And yet here she is, smiling at him almost in the same spot where she threw him out, her eyes transfixed with interest as he reels off for her swings and percentages, net gains and losses.

"Oh, Marcus, that *is* interesting," she says, raising her glass to her lips and stretching out her long handsome legs.

Oh yes. I forgot. As well as everything else, the bell doesn't work. Which is why Terry is standing now upon the doorstep, a look of aggravation upon his face, a bottle clutched in one hand and the other clenched and raised for a final thunderous knock.

"It's Terry we've got to watch out for," she said. "He's an unpleasant, creepy little bastard who pretends to like women when he doesn't. But he's the one with the say down there so I've got to get him on my side.

"Be nice to him, Rose," she said.

• • •

"Terry. And Dorothea. I'm afraid the bell doesn't work. Not been knocking long, I hope."

In the bedroom, Dorothea bends double on white high shoes, peering in the dressing table mirror by the light of a badly shaded low-watt bulb. Her slightly too tight pink dress with its little lace collar rides up as she bends and pats more powder on an already deeply beiged nose. She puts on lipstick, working her lips together thoughtfully before dropping it back in her white plastic bag which she closes with a snap.

"Right," she says playfully, like a girl. "I'm ready."

Downstairs she sips her sherry on the sofa next to Terry, her legs placed primly together, her eyes lifting continually and admiringly to him between the quick, low, inquisitive looks she darts at Jo and Marcus and myself.

She looks like a woman who needs assurances, who needs to know the landmarks are in place. She looks like a woman who approves of parties where husbands arrive with wives but leave them hastily in one room to join the men in the other. She looks like a woman who will call Marcus Jo's "boyfriend," who will wonder, idly, how long they have been "going out," who, scrabbling around for words to describe to her own satisfaction the relationship, will turn up some unwieldy and old-fashioned, some rusty with age and disuse, some she has trouble remembering from a time, hazy now and indistinct, before she was married.

And I see now why Marcus is here and why Jo fusses, ostentatiously, around him.

"Another glass of wine, Marcus... some more Bombay mix, Marcus... sit over here, Marcus."

Passing behind him as he sits in an armchair by the sofa, she lays two friendly hands upon his shoulders, palms down, intimating an old and enduring relationship, one to be relied upon and respected, one not to be underrated, one which like an old house plant pushed aside into a corner might explode one day into glorious highly coloured flowers after many years of dull undistinguished foliage.

At which moment there is a second knock at the door.

• • •

They stand upon the doorstep like strangers, like two actors chosen for their resemblance to the characters they are about to play.

She wears a smart black dress and an expensive new cream jacket. The old frizzy perm has been lopped away, leaving in its place a cap of shining dark hair, cut very short and standing in spikes on top of her head.

Over her shoulder is a shiny new leather handbag, hanging neat and flat and entirely free of bulges.

And yet it's not Margaret who causes the exclamation.

"Good God, Martin. You've grown a beard."

"Strangest thing," Paul said to me once, when I was lying in his arms. "Jo hates beards. I mean hates. Fanatical about them. Wouldn't speak to me. Literally wouldn't speak to me when I grew one for a while. She said they were a throwback. The last pathetic attempt by the modern male to become a caveman again."

And now here's Martin standing in her hall with a beard, with this declaration of intent sprouted upon his chin, to be her lover no longer, to be instead husband to Margaret, Margaret whom he met when she was a student teacher and he was in the shipyard, working for the union, studying at night-school and carefully nursing a new, sparse but quite promising bristle.

"Hallo, Rose," he says, pushing past me in the doorway and squeezing my arm in an ebullient fashion.

"Don't you like it? It's the new macho me."

Martin looks like a man persuaded that he has passed through a dark night of the soul, a man satisfied he has at last located his own salvation. Martin looks like a man who has decided that all that happened happened for the best. Martin looks like a man who has decided he wants to be married to his wife again.

There's a bravado about him, not just in the beard but in the brazen quality of the stare that accompanies the stride as he enters the lounge, the stare that says that he has come with his wife whom he loves, and he is happy and let him who dares step forward and say it is not so.

"Marcus," he says, singing out the name with deliberate

avuncularity and good humour. "And how are we doing in the polls?"

"Trailing," says Marcus pleasantly, raising his head from the desk lamp he is mending. "Yes, trailing I'm afraid," he says, bending his head once more to his work.

Something else about Margaret has changed.

She ignores Martin. No, it is more than that. She seems entirely cut off from him and, indeed, from all those around her, as if she is existing in one of those transparent bubbles which those lacking immunity live in, when what they are will not allow them to survive in the world.

She sits next to Dorothea now on the end of the sofa, not troubling to hide a crippling boredom. I have it. What she is doing is declining to make an effort, which in her, the MP's wife, is frankly quite shocking.

I see that Margaret cannot be relied upon tonight to play the part of wife of Martin. Not tonight. Or maybe any other night.

Margaret will no longer laugh dutifully at his bad jokes, play the pleasant wife to garner his votes. She will no longer put herself selflessly in the firing line of his bores and his nuisances, head off the phone-in freaks, the newspaper letter-writers, the cranks and the crackbrains.

No, Margaret has served notice on all that.

Tonight she shows us the future. How it will be. Tonight she is merely a guest at a dinner party, a guest like all the rest, free of responsibilities, a conscript, forced to take the King's shilling like them while fantasising at the same time of all the other places it would be better to be.

And I understand and say "Dinner is served" from the archway, in sympathy, in that ridiculous over-bright way you say it where you wish you were not, with people with whom you wish not to be, half in horror, half in relief, thinking, "Well, here we are, dinner at least. Time must have passed."

They dawdle through the archway to the dining room like members of an official party, disparate and bored and brought together by expedience.

At the head of the procession Martin and Terry stroll

like elder statesmen, dark-suited and serious, talking in shortforms.

There's something a little lost about Terry. Something a little unhappy. He's schoolmasterly and dull, a man condemned forever by his own finer feelings to come to terms with a world which is not really his.

"Of course," he says to Martin, firmly re-settling his old-fashioned silver-and-black spectacles, "women are doing *very* well in teaching now."

But his voice, worn flat and dull with a weakness for shouted sarcasms, makes the words sound forced and insincere and so he tries again.

"And of course," he says, "they're doing frightfully well in the party."

Beside him Martin struts, already a little drunk. He has sung Jo's praises to Terry, and it has made him feel benevolent and fatherly and as though he has somehow set the world to rights. But more than that, it has made him feel important and prized for his opinion and rather more himself again.

"And so they should," he says, his voice bluff and forceful. "What we want. More women MPs. They've worked for it. Kept the party together. Look at Jo. Like I told you. Simply couldn't have done it without her."

Behind them, several paces behind them, Margaret walks, as a female interpreter might walk, out of the limelight, glad to be alone for a moment, but still a crooked finger away from the heads of state.

And behind them Jo and Marcus, the jokers in the pack, interested only in each other, emerging from the archway like lovers from the tunnel of love at the end of the pier, she still gushing with gratefulness over the mended desk lamp.

"Thank you *so* much, Marcus. Really I've been quite lost without it."

I said to her once, "I'll take that lamp to be mended if you like." But she said, "Don't bother. I never use it."

We have finished the melon and the goulash is out on the plates by the time Dorothea is finally discovered to be missing.

At the moment of the discovery, though, she explodes

through the archway breathless and ungainly in her little girl's dress, scraping her high heels noisily on the tiled floor.

"I got locked in the loo," she says, letting out a high-pitched little giggle which corkscrews her body with merriment as she looks around the table.

In the silence her smile begins to fade and she lowers herself, face already flushing, onto her seat.

She pats her curls and purses her lips and then reaches back behind her to slip the handles of her white plastic bag over the delicately carved knobs of Jo's elegant high-backed dining chairs.

Opposite her the hostess' mouth has dropped open. She stares at Dorothea as if trying to place her on the evolutionary scale.

"What are you working on at the moment, Marcus?" I ask hastily to fill up the appalled and embarrassed silence.

"A little light relief, actually," says Marcus. "We've been doing a survey on adultery."

Afterwards she will banish him a second time from the house, saying icily, "Ten out of ten, Marcus, for your choice of subject for conversation at dinner. So carefully thought out. So uncontroversial."

Now she chokes noisily on her first forkful of goulash, reaching for her glass as her face deepens to a fiery red from coughing.

Opposite her, Martin curses as the goblet of wine which he knocked over as Marcus spoke washes around his baked potatoes and salad like a tide.

Along from him, Margaret leans back and smiles with cold unashamed amusement while at her side Dorothea scrabbles a Kleenex from her bag and blows her nose with all-consuming concentration.

As for me, I lower my head to my food, resisting the temptation to cover my face with my hands, so that it is left to Terry, who else but Terry, to clear his throat, give an extra forceful thrust to his glasses and ask quite calmly as if he were discussing a poll on the user-friendly qualities of rival softwares, "Oh really? Any interesting conclusions?"

• • •

Marcus has missed all of this, concerned as he is to place exactly the correct amount of butter and pepper upon his baked potato.

Now he lifts trailing whisps of salad, apparently unaware of the mayhem around him.

"Yes, very interesting, actually. We may be witnessing something of a minor moral revolution."

He clasps his hands together, jamming them under his nose as he always does when about to launch upon a detailed explanation of one of his surveys.

"More salad, anyone?" calls Jo gaily. "Don't start Marcus on his polls, Terry, we'll be here all night."

Her voice is high with a hard edge of panic. She rises to her feet and waves her arms around frantically passing salad and baked potatoes to those who no longer require them.

At the same time she presses the heel of her right court shoe down upon the toe of Marcus' left moccasin but to absolutely no avail.

"Jo finds my surveys a bit tedious sometimes," he confides to the table, smiling relentlessly. "But really, Jo," he says, turning to her, "I think even you'll find this interesting."

He clears his throat and leans forward, massaging his hands together beneath his nose and speaking earnestly.

"You see, basically we did the survey because the advertising world needed to know if adultery is still a taboo subject. They've gone about as far as they can go with Mr and Mrs and the two kids, and anyway it's hard to make happy families glamorous or sophisticated. They needed to know if they would offend public morality taking a rather more risqué approach to some product advertising. You know, intimating the woman wearing the new perfume is having an affair, possibly with the man with the racy-looking new car."

"And would they be offended?" asks Terry politely, forced to take another baked potato from the bowl pushed at him by Jo's insistent hand.

"Not at all. It's quite extraordinary. The results showed that the overwhelming amount of people don't see adultery as being wrong in the ordinary sense of the word. That is, they separate it quite explicitly from the other sins. They don't, for instance, regard cheating on your wife in the same light as other forms of cheating, fiddling the tax man for instance."

"Do go on, Marcus," says Jo, smiling dangerously and sitting down to pick at her own baked potato as though it had suddenly become highly radioactive.

"There you are," he says waggishly, "I knew you'd be interested. No, the thing is, people feel that adultery as a sin is somehow different. Excusable.

"Apart from anything else," he says, lowering his hands at last to pick up his knife and fork, "it seems to me the results are of particular interest to politicians."

There's a feeling around the table among those who know that a die has been cast.

Martin, for instance, stares gloomily into his glass, his plate of food untouched, while Margaret plays with her salad.

And so it falls to Terry again to speed destiny on its way.

"How do you mean?" he says, applying himself with some force to his second dried-up baked potato.

"Well, it's obvious, isn't it? All the fuss in the papers every time a cabinet minister or even a humble MP is found to have committed adultery. The fact is that our results show that the public doesn't care. One of the questions specifically asked was whether those interviewed would still vote for an MP of their choice who was publicly convicted of having an affair. The answer was a surprisingly resounding 'yes.' So it looks like the papers have got it wrong. After all. When you think about it, the Kennedy name doesn't seem to have suffered even though we all know now that JFK was screwing around at the White House."

"Let us now praise famous men and forget about their peccadilloes?"

"Exactly, Rose. And you know why people don't care?"

"Do tell us, Marcus." It is Jo again, her voice heavy with resignation.

"Because everybody's doing it."

"Let him who is without sin...?"

"Right again, Rose. Do you know that seventy-five per cent of married men we interviewed admitted to committing adultery and sixty-eight per cent of women? And here's the interesting thing. While the male figure has stayed pretty much constant for the last fifteen years, the female figure has gone up and up.

"Anyway, old man," he finishes with a flourish, looking at Martin, a forkful of goulash trembling in the air, "the message is do your worst. The public will still vote for you."

Astonishing, all things considered, that Marcus should try his hand at wit again. For the truth is the words are meant to be witty.

I can see that by the look of innocent, earnest concentration on his face, the same look I am sure that stared into the screen of his word processor the night he constructed his marriage proposal.

He means the words to be a mere confection, the sort of witty social nicety he reads about in books, the sort that fall lightly into the air and engender gentle rustles of appreciative laughter around the table.

Unfortunately, though, he speaks them with the peculiar emphasis that bedevils witticisms spoken by those unaccustomed to their use, and this plus his look of studied concentration weighs them down so that they land in Martin's lap leaden and overblown and loaded with the potential for misapprehension.

Marcus, you see, is entirely innocent. She packed him off so quickly out of the house that night he never got the chance to ask, "Whose baby?" And he never knew about Martin. No one knew about Martin. Apart perhaps from Margaret.

But the trouble is that Martin knows about Marcus. At the time he was flattered by his presence, flattered at this mild unspoken game of make-believe jealousy he thought Jo was playing. And so he was overbearingly friendly to Marcus when he turned up with her at party functions, treating him with amused condescension.

But those were the old days. And love is a horse-race. And now Martin is out on the rails.

And Marcus's words come at him like a faceful of flying mud.

●　●　●

He rises to his feet slowly, face flushed with drink, a man in pain, a man who knows that his moment has arrived and more likely than not he will be found wanting.

His eyes are blurred and damp with unshed tears, tears trembling behind the fringe of his lower lashes, a flood of tears held back by the leaky, sodden sandbags of a pathetic but miraculous dignity, tears of shame and desperation, tears the richer for being unshed, tears for himself and for Margaret and for Jo, tears for Danny and Janet and Micky, tears for a flag on a bed and for hair lopped away, tears for a handbag and hope in a beard, tears for a drawing and a locked bathroom door, real tears for real people. Tears of hopeless, disorderly, inadequate love.

He crushes a napkin in a knuckle white with strain as he stares at Marcus, and when he speaks the words emerge ruptured and strangled as if broken on a wheel of misery lodged in his throat.

"You bastard," he says.

Perhaps if Martin was sober he would see that Marcus is aghast and bewildered. Perhaps he would see that Marcus strains back in his seat and fiddles nervously with his napkin and looks around him helplessly with the old myopic stare of one who finds himself abused by those who should have been amused.

But Martin sees none of these things, not only because he is drunk but also because his view is clouded by memories, so that looking at Marcus he sees only his own suspicions.

"You bastard," he says again, leaning threateningly towards him.

"Sit down, Martin, for God's sake, and shut up," says Jo angrily, slapping down her serviette on the table.

And then it happens. Margaret, who has sat silent all evening watching what has gone on around her like one watching a performance in which she has no part, raises her head proudly, as a bull might raise his head at a matador, and speaks.

Her voice is a hiss of steaming hate, her eyes two white-hot suns searing into Jo.

"How dare you speak to my husband like that," she says.

. . .

For a moment there is total silence. No knife scrapes upon plate or hand reaches for glass. Around the table we wait as if caught, all of us, in a freeze frame, waiting to be freed by the projectionist's finger.

"I'm sorry," says Jo to Margaret.

Her voice is deep and quite free of the irony that runs through it like a seam. She speaks as if they are alone in the room, as if the two words are a code and many-layered and say many things which now do not need to be said between them. Around her lips there is the hint of a smile, a smile altogether devoid of malice or mockery, a smile more of admiration, like the smile of a hunter caught in his own trap reflecting with pleasure on the cunning of his prey.

"I do beg your pardon, Martin," she says, turning to smile at him as he lowers himself on his seat.

"Really, Marcus, what a tasteless remark. Cheese and biscuits, anyone?"

Later, in the bedroom, lifting Margaret's jacket from the bed, I cannot resist draping its expensive softness around my shoulders.

"Nice, isn't it," she says, her reflection appearing behind mine in the mirror on the wardrobe door.

"It was Martin's apology. I always buy good stuff when Martin apologises. I know it has to last. I did well this time. I even got a new handbag."

Her voice is low and ironic but honest amusement dances in her eyes.

"Why do you stay with him?"

"Why?"

She draws the word out, letting it rise first and then break and fall, like the plummeting trails of a firework, scattering around us on the bedroom floor garish sparks of bitterness, disillusionment and anger but softer streaks too of affection, pity and understanding.

"Because I think he's no worse than the rest. No better and no worse. Why go looking for another one at my time of life?"

She says it matter-of-factly, without regret, as of a business to be stated.

"Actually," she says, "compared to most, I rather like him."

"So do I. But still..."

"But still, why put up with him when I know he's been having an affair for the past four years? It is four years, isn't it? Well... there's the children."

"I see."

"No. With respect, I don't think you do. I don't think, if you've never had children, you can ever really 'see,' and I don't mean to be patronising. It's just that you can't know the one fundamental truth that comes to women who have children, that it's children that count in a marriage, not men."

She takes the jacket gently from my shoulders and slips it around her own.

"Men," she says, lifting the bright new handbag from the bed. "We fall in love with them and then they make us pregnant and we discover the truth, that they were only ever a means to an end.

"I've always thought," she says laughing, "if they discover a way to produce children without men, they'll be pretty much finished as a sex."

16

I feel like a prisoner in a small cell, a cell whose every corner I know as I know the creases and crevices of my own body. He leaves me alone here, staring at the wall, for many hours, for many days. Food appears and I eat it, tasting nothing, with only my belly to tell me I am full. And then suddenly here he is before me, strolling up and down, amused and wicked, leaning back in a chair and smiling at me, talking and smoking a cigarette. Pretending I have never been alone.

"Did you know seventy-five per cent of married men admit to having had an affair and sixty-eight per cent of women?"

• • •

"We're learning, Rose, we're learning," as Jo once said to me. "You're so naïve, you think women are different from men. You think we're better somehow. More moral. *Nicer.* But it's not true. We're just weaker, still, and less adventurous, with a lot more to learn. But we will learn to be like men and when we do we'll be a hundred per cent better at it, tougher, more selfish, more ruthless. Because with them it's innate and growing weaker with each generation. But with us it's self-taught and growing stronger all the time."

"No, I didn't know that."
"And did you know that one in three marriages now ends in divorce?"

He stubs his cigarette out. The smile will not fade upon his face. He will not be moved. He will not be caught out. He will not be forced into a scene.
"This stuff's not on the syllabus, is it, Rose?" he says easily, not looking at me, pushing the cigarette harder into the ashtray.
"Light relief," I say, smiling back.

You see, I'll do anything now. I'm not ashamed. I've lost all that. I know the end is in sight. But I want him. I want him here. Which is why I called him. At home.

"I'm sorry to bother you but is Paul there? It's Rose. One of his students... In books they always hang up when the wife answers."
"Luckily we're not in books, Rose."
"Look, I need a break. I'm not feeling so good. It's the revision. It's getting on top of me. There are problems. I can't get the books that I want. I'm beginning to panic. I need to relax. Let's have dinner. At the Admiral. We'll have a good bottle of wine and watch the boats. Please, Paul, please."

He said "yes" to placate me. I knew it. At the other end of the phone I could hear the whirrs and clicks of his brain. It's all getting too much... she's an attractive woman of course... it's been fun... but it hasn't worked out... I never thought she was the clinging type...It's unfortunate...I'll have to be careful...after the exams...I'll let her down gently....

"I can't get there till late."

"It doesn't matter. We'll eat at home instead. I'll buy some pasta. Get some wine. We can sit in the window. Look at the river. Never mind if you can't stay long."

You see, I'll do anything.

"You sound shocked. You think it's high?"

"Of course, don't you? Every third marriage failing? Ending up on the rocks?"

"To be honest, it doesn't strike me as a figure of much significance. If it was two in three or even three in three, it still wouldn't make any difference."

"What do you mean? Difference to what?"

"Look, Rose, of course the statistic keeps going up. It's bound to. People's expectations of marriage keep going up because of the explosion in popular culture. Books and films and television tell us a happy marriage is a right now, whatever 'happy marriage' means. Now I don't know if it's a good thing or a bad thing but that's the way it is. But, whatever, people still go on getting married just the same."

"Well, of course, and that's what's so stupid, don't you see. People marry too young with absurdly romantic expectations and then, even sillier, marry again with all the same expectations a second and a third time. And, for heaven's sake, they marry exactly the same sort of people who failed them the first time."

"You want to take our romantic expectations away from us, Rose? Surely it's the only thing that keeps us going."

He is leaning towards me, his hands cupped around his wine glass. He has the warm, earnest look of concern upon his face, the one that I like to pretend belongs only to me, even though I know it is as indiscriminate as Sandra's smile, and he so free with his favours that I share this my special look with half the students in town.

Still, in the half-light he looks so beautiful to me that I flounder and lose my thread, "No...not exactly...but..."

"Look, you say one in three marriages fail and the word

'fail' is all-important to you. And I'll grant you they do 'fail' in the eyes of the divorce courts, but what does 'fail' mean? Does it cover twelve years of a relatively contented marriage or twenty as easily as it covers two brief unhappy years? And you don't mention the two out of three marriages that succeed and give everyone the hope to keep trying because for you they pale into insignificance compared to the one out of three that fails."

I won't look at him. There's a lump in my throat and I want to cry. I wish I had never started this argument. I can see out through the mist on the water to the river mouth, to where it widens into the sea, and I can see where the argument began and where it will end.

"You see, Rose, you speak as someone who has never married. You judge the rest of us harshly, you who have never tried. When you see a marriage fail you assume that people must have set out upon it lightly. Some do, of course. But for most it's a romantic commitment almost religious in its sincerity and seriousness, a striving for an ideal, the ideal that you can merge your life and being with someone else's. Maybe it's an impossible ideal, maybe it's absurd, maybe it's not even desirable, but nonetheless it is an ideal, perhaps the greatest ideal the human race possesses. And even when we fail, the ideal is still there. Perhaps it grows even stronger when we fail, which is why we try again and again."

I would tell him now if I could, if my throat would let me speak, if I could be sure I could keep back the tears.

I would tell him what I saw and what his sister saw that I had seen.

I saw it all, you see.

"OK then. One quick goodnight because Daddy's busy. And then bed."

I saw him turn from the desk and lift her upon one knee while sweeping the hair away from a damp little forehead pressed at the other.

"And do you know what he said, Daddy . . . ?"

"I didn't. I didn't. She's lying."

"Shush now. That's not nice. No quarrelling. Time for bed. Daddy has lots to do."

And then I saw myself, walking towards him, felt my shoes clattering upon the polished boards, felt the weight of her body on my hip and the wonderful trustful curling of a clutch of tiny fingers.

"Night-night," I heard him say. "Night-night" in charming baby talk, bending back once more across his books.

"Aren't you sorry," I say to him, to the river, "aren't you sorry you never had children?"

But he doesn't answer. Just shakes his head and says, "Well," drawing it out, long and non-committal, and drains off his glass of wine and later takes his leave, unhindered and strangely unprotested, pursing his lips and nodding his head in farewell, and closes the door carefully behind him and walks at a steady pace to the car where he lets himself in and flicks on the lights, which sweep across the window in an arc as he pulls away, catching the shadow sitting there, silent and still, a warm human being turning slowly beneath his spell to cold inanimate stone.

"Rose?"
"Jennifer?"

I don't remember the night fading into the early pearly grey of the river dawn and on into this dull May morning and yet it must have done so for here I am, still in the window, talking on the phone to Jennifer.

"Are you all right, Rose?"
"What time is it?"
"It's ten o'clock. What's the matter?"
"Nothing. I was working late. I must have fallen asleep. Over my books."
"How's it going?"
"Not good. I can't get the books that I want. Have you been to the library? It's almost empty. Just spaces where the books used to be. I shall have to go into town today to see if I can buy what I want."

But I can tell she isn't listening and so I ask, "How are things with you?"

She says, "I'm tired. David and I have been up half the night talking. It can't go on, Rose."

I say, "I'm sorry, Jennifer," but at the other end of the phone she clicks her tongue with impatience.

"No. You don't understand. I mean it can't go on with Francie. I told him he simply had to get out. Get it over with. He agreed. He knows I'm right. He's going to tell her, tonight, when she gets home from work.

"Really, Rose," she says, "I'm thinking of her as much as myself.

"Actually," she says, "you can be the first to know. We've decided to get married."

After that she begins to talk quickly, as if afraid I might interrupt her, as if afraid I might spoil the moment.

She speaks in her old voice, the old soft voice that sighs down the line from the past, from a time before there was David. Only now it seems no longer to belong to her, as if she has assumed it, as the wicked stepmother might assume the voice of Snow White, taking the sweetest of her sentiments and turning them cloying and artificial and sickly.

"It probably seems strange to you, Rose, us wanting to get married. But we've found out that we're both rather old-fashioned people. Old romantics really, I suppose. But we think if you love someone you have to make a commitment."

"I can see that, Jennifer."

"He's so talented, Rose. But he needs looking after. Sometimes he even forgets to eat if there's no food put in front of him."

"That happens to me too, Jennifer."

"I want to look after him, you see, Rose."

"That's nice, Jennifer."

"I'm so happy, Rose."

"I'm so glad, Jennifer."

Now I'll tell you something about love. Love separates the weak from the strong. Love is the great testing ground. Love is Everest without oxygen, Niagara Falls in a barrel and the Atlantic in an open boat. Love is the bull ring and the battlefield, the submachine-gun and the face of the shark. Love is where some screw their courage to the sticking place and others slink away into the night.

Which is why I fear for you now, Francie.

I fear for your thin black-stockinged legs beneath your tight pelmet skirt disappearing up the winding spiral staircase in search of my books.

I fear for your tiny pointed toes and your little sharp-nailed hands and the spikes of your fringe above the fearsome black rings of your eyes. I fear for all of your brittle little matchstick-girl, about to be snapped.

Listen to me, Francie. Love finds out the weak. I know about these things. It has found me out already.

I thought Jennifer was weak. But I was blinded by the softness of her eyes, by her silky hair before the fire. I sat on her velvet sofa and ate from her frail antique tablecloth and so thought her tender and vulnerable and as destructible as them. But I was wrong. God help you, Francie. Jennifer is none of these things.

No, Jennifer is strong, Francie. Jennifer is tough. Jennifer is sturdy and built to stay the course. You're a twig, little match-girl, but Jennifer's a trunk. You're a thread but Jennifer's a rod of steel.

Oh Francie Francie Francie. Beneath your jutting sharpness, your spikes, your pins, your points, you're fleece and down and snowflake.

But behind her fragility, Jennifer is flint, Jennifer is axe-head, Jennifer is broken glass and bayonet and blade and razor's edge.

Listen to me, Francie.

Twenty years ago, in an office all dark green and grimy with the years, they gave me a book, a special book, a book that showed me the way to beat the words out properly upon the old black upright typewriter.

"Always remember," said the book, "a man marries a woman and a woman is married to a man."

But that was twenty years ago. Times change, Francie. And Jennifer is going to marry David.

I can see things, Francie, things for David, special things peeping from a bag. I can see fresh asparagus and salmon steaks and good white wine. But too late, Francie, too late.

For I am a sage, Francie. I am Cassandra. I can tell for-
tunes, I can look into the future. And I can see green asparagus gone grey and blush-pink salmon in a bin and a
bottle rolling upon a table and weeping its last drops of
wine upon the floor. And I can see David at the door saying, "I have to talk to you, Francie."

Don't go home, Francie, don't go home. Take your asparagus and your salmon and your wine and go to friends. Go
to women friends, Francie. Hole up there. Claim sanctuary.
Because David wants to talk to you. God help you, David
wants to talk to you, Francie.

David wants to sit down in front of you, his hands
caught at his loins, clasping and unclasping in what he
believes is love and understanding.

He wants to say, "You don't know how much this hurts
me, Francie," and having convinced himself of his own distress wants to drop easily into the past tense, leaving you
stranded in the present.

He wants to say, "We've meant so much to each other,
Francie."

And then David wants to smile at you comfortingly from
the past, while here before him, in the present, the colour
drains away from your face and your shopping bag flops
gently to the floor.

And then he wants to tell you about Jennifer. He wants
to tell you that he loves Jennifer, which perhaps may be
true, and that Jennifer loves him, which sad to say is past
all possible doubting.

And then like a being from another world able to stride
through the galaxies or a giant bounding from peak to
mountain peak, he wants to leap like a madman from the
past to the future and tell you he wants to marry Jennifer.

Listen to me, Francie. Sometimes love is so simple.
Sometimes life gets it right. Sometimes when destiny rolls
the dice, two sixes come up side by side.

Jennifer and David, you see, were meant for each other.

Look, Jennifer can make pastry and cheese soufflés
which don't sink in the middle. Jennifer washes sweaters

that don't shrink and puts zips in and does buttonholes. Pot plants *grow* for Jennifer. Cats purr. Children run into her arms. She can wallpaper round doors and paint without dripping, and frankly she has other advantages too. To be blunt, poets are badly paid, Francie. Which all makes Jennifer the perfect wife for David.

She will read his proofs for him, fill in his tax returns and book his train tickets. She will pack his case for him and take him to the station and hold up the children to kiss him good-bye.

She will appear at his side when needed, beautiful and elegant, making David the envy of other men, and when not required will remain at home, running his life there, so that it closes back around him smoothly and securely and tastefully when he returns from his lecture tours and his tacky little affairs, when he returns home yearning for French cooking and fine wines after too many weeks of fast food and rough red on the road.

All of which Jennifer will know and all of which, strange as it may seem, will not weigh heavily with Jennifer.

Listen, Francie. Hear what the oracle has to say. The oracle says, Love has found you out already, Francie. How much more would it find you out in ten years' time with only two young children for company and a husband handsome and successful and never at home.

For Jennifer was right, you see.

She said to him last night, "Really, David. You have to do it. You have to get it over with. It's best for Francie in the long run."

And she was right, Francie. It is best for you. Best for you it should be Jennifer, Jennifer who is strong where you are weak and who knows her own worth and knows that he will always return. And best for you, Francie, you should not go home.

For strange things may happen if you go home.

I see you now, Francie, waking as if from a dream, to find yourself devoid of all dignity, thin legs spread-eagled in a deep "V" before him, tears running tramlines of black down your face.

I see you staring at him, unable to remove your gaze from his face as if believing that by fixing him with your sorrow you can somehow seal him also to the spot and prevent him rising from his seat and leaving.

I hear you say, "Don't go, David," your eyes and lips swelling together with the misery.

And I hear you saying, "Don't leave me, David," all unashamed of the smudges on your face and the spittle on your lips and the tiny gleam of snot running down from your nose. And I see his dreadful, helpless, hopeless half-gesture of the hands that says, "What can I say, Francie?"

For what can he say, Francie, this man whose business is words, who deals in the best and the most beautiful in the language, but who cannot find among them the ones that he needs to tell you the simple unpoetic truth, that he doesn't want you anymore but wants Jennifer instead?

And what can you say, Francie, to change his mind, sitting there before him, shreds of pride whisper-soft around your ankles? What can you say who will say anything now?

I'll tell you what you'll say, Francie.

You'll say, "Not tonight, David," or, "Just tonight, David," or, "Even if you go tomorrow, David" or any other banalities that spring to mind as you stare up at him, your face blackened and blotchy and unbecoming.

"Look," you will say, clawing at the bag and rolling out your goods upon the floor like a souvenir seller with trinkets before a tourist, "I have salmon and asparagus and good white wine. Not tonight, David, not tonight."

"It's no good, Francie," he'll say. "It's no good," each "no good" piercing like a spear thrust, ripping you open and spewing you out as you crouch before him at his feet.

"No, David, no," you will say, bony knees upon the lino, little white fists drumming a hopeless tattoo upon his jeans.

And then you reach, Francie, reach up, a nervous and delicate touch to his face, this face you thought that you knew but which freezes your finger-tips now as it turns to the face of a stranger.

Look now, Francie, see here in my crystal ball. See the face, Francie, and tell me where you have seen it before. It has stared down at you, Francie, times without number, eyes inches from yours, blank and empty of recognition, full instead of the blind effort, the impersonal striving, the curious detachment of sexual endeavor.

• • •

I know a woman, Francie, who tells a story, laughing, after her fourth glass of whisky, about the politics lecturer she fell in love with as a student, who kissed her on the cheek, courteously, saying things could not continue as before.

I know a woman who went to bed for a week, weeping, but who rose up on the eighth day, stronger and wiser, and booked a ticket for America and went to say good-bye but found in his room instead of him a semi-circle of his students, girl students, who smiled and said, "He'll be here any moment," so that she smiled back and said, "No matter," and reached for the chalk on the tiny shelf beneath the blackboard and began to write, shielding her words with her back.

And when she had finished she signed her name and put the chalk back on the shelf and turned and smiled again and walked out of the room leaving them to read what she had written.

And this is what she wrote, this woman, and this is what he found a moment later when he burst through the door, arms full of papers, charming and all smiles himself, to face a silent room.

"My dear," she wrote. "This is in the nature of good-bye. You have a lovely body and you're wonderful in bed. In fact, if you ever get your cock connected to your brain you could be a sensation."

Strangers, Francie, strangers with strange faces. Strangers playing their own strange game by their own strange rules. And moving the goal-posts, Francie. Once we had to be weak to be loved. Now we have to be strong.

Love is hard, Francie. Love sorts out the weak from the strong. Perhaps one day you'll be strong, Francie. Strong like Jennifer. Strong like Jo. But not yet. You're weak now, Francie. Weak just like me.

Listen to me, Francie. Hear what I say. Don't go home, Francie. Don't go home.

17

SOMETHING is happening to me. All my strength is falling away. I have been struck down by a wasting disease. Its name is Love.

I get out of bed feeling drowsy and heavy from lack of sleep and decide to go for a walk along the riverside. But fifty yards from my door I am overcome with weariness and return to the house soaked to the skin with a misery that seems to seep into my soul and stop up even my very legs.

"I can't sleep, you see. I go to bed at night with my eyelids closing with tiredness, but as soon as I put my head on the pillow, they fly open again as surely as if someone had shone a bright light on my face.

"I can't work either. I pick up the books and put them down again. They surround me in the flat. Piles of them. Accusing me. Books about books. What could be more foolish. And they're not even the right books. But the library is empty and the bookshop didn't have the ones that I wanted."

"You don't need any more books, Rose. You have all the books you need. It's just an excuse."

He is being so patient. He did not want to see me. I knocked upon his door and he called "Come in" sharply, and when he turned, I saw a shadow of vexation cross his face together with one of harassment, hastily disguised.

And now he is penitent. He spoons coffee, instant coffee, into mugs. "No milk, I'm afraid," he says cheerfully. His discarded pen lies upon a pile of examination manuscripts, upon a page of bold childish handwriting and upon a tiny approving tick newly struck against a line which reads, "Conrad's heroes demonstrate the tragic practical consequences of strict adherence to an ideal."

He looks tired, too. His own weariness prevents him from recognising mine. Back in the director's chair he runs a hand through his hair and reaches for his cigarettes.

I love him. Oh I love him.

"It's the oldest excuse in the world. It's happened to all of us. You have all the books that you need but you just don't want to pick them up and get down to work. So you tell yourself you need the one book you haven't got and so put off the evil hour of actually getting started."

"I want a simple book. A simple book without a fancy title. A book with all the answers."

"There's no such book and you know it."

I stare out of the window, not wishing to look at him. I feel dreamy and disconnected and when I hear my words they sound clumsy and imprecise, as if they somehow fail to match the thoughts in my brain. Outside the half-open window a branch dances lightly in the breeze while here inside I stumble from word to lumbering word.

"I'm ill, Paul. I think I'm ill."

"All you need is a good night's sleep. Go to bed early tonight with a couple of hot whiskys."

"No, it's more serious than that." Still I look out of the window, intoning the words now, speaking them without feeling as if they concern someone other than myself.

"Something is happening to me. I think I'm cracking up. I need help. I can't take the exams."

"Nonsense. Never in my life have I met anyone less likely to crack up. You're a thirty-eight-year-old woman who has fended for herself all her life. You're independent, self-reliant. You're just suffering from a burst of exam nerves, that's all."

"Was, Paul, was. That was in the past. I *was* independent and self-reliant. But I've lost all that. I've no strength now. I've lost it. Given it away. Lost it loving you. I've fallen in love with you. Don't you understand? I didn't mean to. It's not my fault. It just happened. But now I love you, Paul, I love you."

Better this way. Better that it's out and over with. Better this than the waiting by the phone. Better this than the churning stomach and the wet palms and the breath acrid with the panic and over-anticipation of love.

And now there is silence. Around me the world seems to have dissolved into soft focus, with only the branch at the window remaining clear and sharp as it drags an unopen bud across the glass like a long derisive finger-nail.

And then he leans forward, lowering his head and grinding his hands lightly together between his knees, like a man about to be called to give evidence who is thinking very carefully about what he will say.

"Rose..." he begins, slowly and thoughtfully, his eyes still cast down upon the floor, his voice flat and dull from the carefully controlled compassion.

And then there is a tap upon the door, a light tap, an unassuming tap, a tap after all these years still devoid of the force of claim and entitlement.

And there before us is Monica.

"Monica, my wife, Monica, Rose, one of my students."

• • •

Monica my wife. Rose my lover. Rose who has moaned in
my arms as you have, Monica. Rose whose gentlest places I
have known as I have known yours, Monica.
Monica, Rose. Rose, Monica.

Strange that there is no pain, only this vagueness, this in-
distinctness as if the world were fading away all around me.
"Rose is having a bad time with her revision, I'm afraid.
She's not feeling well. She can't sleep."
"Oh I *am* sorry."
Extraordinary. I think she is too. Her eyes are warm
with unsuspicious sympathy. Oh how well we have thought
of Monica.
"I had an awful time during my finals. I took pills to send
me to sleep and pills to wake me up. I just about made it to the
end. We went for a celebration drink after the last exam, and I
only managed two lagers before I had to be carried home.
"Do you remember, Paul?" she says, laughing.
He has emptied his eyes of expression and his face between us is cold and polite, and yet her laughter fans the
old smouldering coals of memories into life so that despite
his determination he smiles.

"I cannot say," he said, "I am unhappy with Monica."

"I have to go. I have to go to the library."
"Forget the library," he says, my tutor, my guardian
now, all hearty and twinkle-eyed.
"I've told you. You've got all the books that you need.
Relax. You've put the work in. You're going to be all right.
And don't forget. A couple of tots of whisky before you go to
bed."
"I do hope you feel better. I know how awful it is. Really,
you do have my sympathy."
There's something about Monica. Something happening
around the eyes and the mouth. There's a warmth, a glow,
a pleasure. Old lines, lines from late nights and looking-
glasses and lonely walks across the carpet, hold up a new
happiness upon her face like bare poles beneath a gloriously caparisoned pavilion.
Love sorts out the weak from the strong, and Monica

looks to me like an old campaigner back in the field. She smiles at me as I back towards the door, mindful perhaps of a need to be benevolent in the face of battle. I know that superstition. Once I helped old ladies across the road in an impenitent attempt to get the gods to smile on Paul and me.

"Thank you. So nice to have met you, Monica."

"And you, Rose. And you."

Coming out together a few minutes later, he turns to lock the door, placing the key carefully in his pocket before ushering her to the top of the stairs with an old, friendly, well-practised hand.

Watching from the landing above, I see her lift her eyes to him, responding to the hand with an older smile of pragmatic, well-tempered affection.

Walking down the stairs together, their bodies incline a little towards each other, as if by habit, like trees or bushes, bent the same way over the years, swayed and buffeted by the same winds.

"I cannot say," he said, "I do not love my wife."

And now pain noses through the world of whiteness around me like the bows of a ship poking through the mist on the river.

I sit on the chair outside of his room where once I sat in my one good suit with my one certificate in my brief-case beside me, where I waited for him to fill in my gaps, where I waited for myself to do the same for him.

Independent, self-sufficient, accustomed to affairs.

Warm. Wasted. Waiting for love.

"Rose."

"Jo."

"Is something the matter?"

"No. Why?"

"What are you doing here? Sitting outside Paul's office. He's gone home."

She is looking at me curiously. Her eyes snap with concern the way they do when people she cares about irritate her.

"I've just seen Paul with Monica. He said I might find

you around here if I hurried. I've got the seat. Quite extraordinary. After all that happened. I've just got home and now I have to turn round and go back again."

"Why?"

"Rose, Rose." She clicks her teeth in fond amusement, an indulgent smile upon her face. "Don't you even listen to the news now? They've announced the election. So I shall be away for the next three weeks at least. I'm just worried about the house. You know how bad it is for burglaries around there. I need someone to house-sit. Any chance of you doing it? It'll be perfect for your revision. It's so quiet there. You'll have the whole house to work in. I know how cramped you get in that tiny flat. And you could send my mail on for me. I'm staying at the family home. I'll give you the address."

She stands the battered brief-case on the parquet and opens it up, not waiting for my reply. As she rummages around inside for pen and paper, she talks without stopping.

"Quite astonishing. Said I was the best candidate. Terry said this. Weaselly Terry. I mean he must have known. God, I'll never forget Dorothea's face during that scene with Martin. Who knows, perhaps Terry took what Marcus said to heart. About people not caring about adultery. Anyway there wasn't a breath of it around. Terry is my agent, if you can believe it, and a bloody good one too. And Dorothea is forever making me tea. Mind you the old man's name helped, of course. Bound to help, having him around when I'm canvassing too.

"Not as good as a pregnant wife, of course," she says, closing the brief-case and rising to her feet, "but we can't have everything."

She peers at me closely as she holds out a sheet of paper and her large old-fashioned front-door key. "Are you sure you're all right?" she asks.

"Yes, I'm all right."

"Mmmm," she says, doubtful and disapproving. "Well ... I won't ask what's wrong. Keep in touch. I'll ring you. How's the revision going, by the way?"

"Not so good. I can't get the books that I want."

"Oh really. Well, I shouldn't worry. You've worked so hard you're bound to be all right. By the way," she says casually as she turns to go. "I'm not supposed to tell anyone this, only family, but then," she gives me a friendly sardonic smile, "you're almost family. Monica's pregnant."

She wants to take me home.

She says, "We'll go round to your flat now and collect your stuff and get you installed." But for once I am firm and I say "no" with a force that surprises her. I tell her, "I have to go to the library. I'll move in tonight."

I shift from foot to foot willing her to go, and when she eventually disappears down the stairs, collapse again back on the chair, putting my head back against the wall and closing my eyes as the pain inches around every last tiny extension of my body.

As my eyes open drowsily, they fix on the typewritten notice on the door opposite.

It says he will be in and he is, sitting at the end of the long inky seminar table, his back against the window, smoking a cigarette and reading a book.

He did not expect to be disturbed and looks up in surprise at the knock and at my head poking around the door.

"Rose," he says, without enthusiasm.

"David," I say with a wide, ingratiating smile.

"Shouldn't you be swotting?" he says, pushing his pebble glasses back on his nose, his tongue lingering in loving mockery over the word. David, who disdained to finish his degree, loves to mock all aspects of academia.

"Probably, but you see, David," I sit down on a chair facing him and place my bag neatly, with schoolgirl care, upon the floor, "I'm really not that bothered about the exams. You see, my writing is the only thing that's really important to me."

"I'm glad to hear that, Rose. It's very refreshing. Frankly some people here..." He grimaces, leaving the sentence unfinished.

"And how is the writing going, Rose?" he asks, leaning back in his chair and peering at me through eyes slanting with smoke and self-satisfaction.

"Frankly, David," I say, shifting my chair a little closer, "that's why I'm here. I need someone to read my novel for me. Someone I trust. Someone whose opinion I value.

Someone," I say, lowering my head in earnestness, "someone who writes themself."

I cast a small conspiratorial look over my shoulder and
around the empty room.

"I've shown it to some people here, of course, but ..."

"Academics," says David tersely.

"Theorists," I reply.

I clear my throat and raise my head as if bracing myself,
as if taking courage.

"You see, I'm at the stage in my writing now where I
need criticism if I am to progress. But I have to have it
from someone whose work I respect, from someone who I
know will understand what I'm trying to do, someone who
understands the challenges and the possibilities, someone
who understands ... *excitement.*"

I clasp my hands fervently. He nods but remains silent,
lifting his cigarette to his lips to wreathe smoke around
the mask of his inscrutability.

I move my clasped hands humbly to my knees.

"Like everyone, I've always admired your work. Your poetry is so utterly stripped, so stark, so absolute, so ..."

"Elemental?"

"Oh yes, elemental. Absolutely elemental. And then, of
course, when Jennifer told me about your idea for the
novel ..."

"You like it?"

"Brilliant."

He takes a last drag on his cigarette and stubs it out
firmly in the lid of his tobacco tin, which he is using as an
ashtray.

Leaning back, his chair creaking loudly in the silence,
he places a thoughtful, magisterial finger upon his lips,
staring at me without blinking for a long moment.

And then with an air of having considered me and having come down finally in my favour, he reaches slowly for
the bottom of the tobacco tin. Plunging the fingers of his
right hand into the candy-floss of brown, he stops suddenly
and theatrically to raise his eyes to mine.

"Time to take the novel by the throat, Rose," he says in a
sonorous voice which rings out emptily around the room.

"David ..." I say helplessly, my hands clasping and unclasping at my knee, my sentence dwindling away in admiration.

"The days are gone when we can churn out this sort of thing and expect to be taken seriously," he says, removing his hand from the tin to toss contemptuously towards me the paperback which he had been reading.

It skids along the table top turning full circle several times, finally landing in my lap with the front cover staring up at me.

"Actually," he said roguishly, "he wrote a novel about the affair."

He gets up from his seat then and walks backwards and forward before the window, stabbing the air with the freshly made roll-up as if lecturing to an audience.

"We're children of the cinema. We can fill in the gaps for ourselves now. We don't need all this tedious narrative. All this getting up and going out and closing doors behind us. That's for the Victorians. The modern reader doesn't need it. He doesn't want it. He's sophisticated. Adaptable. Wants to be given a job to do. Wants to take some form of responsibility for the plot himself. Doesn't want to be spoon-fed in this ridiculous fashion."

I nod and say "yes" and "of course" and "absolutely" at intervals, and in the end he exhausts himself and sits back down, an expression of relief and satisfaction upon his face.

"Well anyway, David," I say, reaching down into my bag to bring up my manuscript, which I lay on the table before him. "I'd be so grateful ... if you wouldn't mind."

"I'll start straight away, Rose."

"No rush, David," I say, getting up and lifting my bag from the floor. "Absolutely no rush. I know you're busy with your own work.

"Here's your book," I say, pushing it back across the table towards him.

"Take it. Take it," he says, waving it away. "I've read enough. Read it. Tell me what you think. Frankly I can't believe people are still writing this stuff."

"Naturalistic junk," I say shortly.

"Booker fodder," he replies.

"Thank you, David," I say quietly, backing respectfully to the door. "Thanks for everything."

Lowering my head, I pull it open, passing halfway through before finally turning, my hand upon the door-knob.

"By the way, David," I say, as if with an afterthought, "I don't suppose by any chance you'd have any dope on you, would you?"

18

I told David, "It's the only thing that makes me sleep, and I haven't been sleeping."

He looked away for a moment, drumming his fingers lightly on the table. Then he reached down to the floor for his grubby white canvas bag, which he lifted and stood on the table, taking from it a plastic pouch.

"It's good stuff," he said, unfolding it delicately. "Not for the faint-hearted."

"I could do Niagara Falls in a barrel," I said. "Give me as much as you've got."

. . .

He did well on the deal, of course. But still I smiled at
him just the same. I said, "Thanks again, David. Give my
love to Jennifer. Oh and congratulations. Really, I think
you were made for each other."

It's a long time since I smoked dope. The last time I
think was the stuff Luis pressed into my hand in the jeep
outside the station.
"It'll help with the pain, Rose," he said. And it did.
I smoked it alone in my hotel room. Under its spell I
grew confident that he would call until the room grew
empty and echoing with the sound of the silent phone,
when I found all of a sudden that I no longer cared.
And so I called Luis at the hacienda to tell him, and when
he answered the phone I could hear the sound of the accordion and the guitars, and I had to shout a little to make him
hear.
"Everything's all right, Luis," I said.
And so it was with David's dope. It was dark and sticky
and very sweet-smelling, and with the first breath I felt
the pain draw away, the pain that exploded in my head the
moment Jo told me Monica was pregnant.

"But I thought..."
"What did you think, Rose? Did you think Paul and
Monica did not make love any longer? Yes, Paul and Monica have sex together, they go to the supermarket together
too, and make out their Christmas card list together, they
buy new cars together, sometimes go out into the country
to look at large houses they cannot afford together. Because they are married, Rose. Because they are husband
and wife and such things husbands and wives do together,
such things that survive long after the things they do separately have been forgotten."
She took a step towards me. In her eyes I could see a
flinty humorous affection.
"All that fuss," she said indulgently.
"You were never in any danger of breaking up my dear
brother and his wife. I tried to tell you but you didn't want
to listen. You wanted so much to think you were different.
After all, *he* couldn't do it." She spoke his name from the

corner of a sardonic smile. "And if he couldn't do it, what hope had you?"

She was right, of course. I see that now. I see it all now. If he couldn't do it, what hope had I. I've read his novel, you see. Not once but many times, over and over, carrying it with me everywhere, walking up the stairs to bed with it, to fall asleep across it, to be woken by it scraping my face on the pillow first thing in the morning, taking it to the bathroom to soak in the old claw-foot tub with it, or to the kitchen to munch a handful of musty nuts with it, or a soft biscuit, or to drink a cup of tea with it while reading it to Che Guevara.

"As it happens," he said, "it's a very good novel." And it is. It's a warm novel. Like all the best novels. It makes me laugh. It also makes me want to weep.

I can see why David hated it. People do open and close doors in it. They have the decency to start at the beginning in it and to proceed in an orderly fashion through to the finish in it, and further cannot resist rounding things off nicely in it by ending the affair in the same little Italian restaurant where it all began.

So here they sit, on this his last night, at the very same table, but dining too early now, surrounded by office workers and late night shoppers, awkward in the absence of ambience like actors unused to playing tragedy at a matinee.

It was midsummer when they began the affair. Now it is winter, with the snow thick upon the pavements.

She looks at her watch. She is nervous. She says, "I could not reach him. He will be worried," adding vaguely, as if by way of explanation, "with the snow."

"Monica," he says, "you're not listening to me. I'm asking you to leave him to come with me."

She will not look at him. Seems to flutter a little. Drops her fork and calls for vinaigrette so that he too becomes agitated, suspecting she would prefer he had not spoken.

"Monica," he says, "listen to me. I love you and I believe you love me."

She lifts her glass, shaking her head in listless irritation. "Oh love," she says, "love..."

And then she becomes a Monica he does not recognise, a

Monica who fixes him with eyes that do not seem to know him, who talks about herself as if even she were a stranger.

"Perhaps I might go with you," she says, musing, as if she proposed a day in the country or a trip to the shops.

"Perhaps I might go with you if you offered me something different. Something new. But only love..."

He suspects now the earth of trembling and perhaps of preparing itself to open and swallow him up. He lays down his knife and fork in anticipation.

"Monica," he says, "I don't understand." And he doesn't, for bewilderment mingles in his voice with the hurt, lightening its texture and raising its tone.

"Doesn't it mean anything to you, Monica? What we had together?" he asks.

"Yes, it does. But the extraordinary thing is it doesn't seem to mean enough. That is, it doesn't seem to make any difference."

She is still now, all the fluttering and listlessness quite gone. She speaks sadly, but what hurts him more is that what she says appears to leave her at peace.

"I'm surprised that it doesn't make a difference, but it doesn't and I don't know why. Perhaps it's just a lack of faith on my part, but the truth is I can see no point in leaving him. Perhaps the truth is that within the terms of what is possible, I really am quite happy."

Her words tear into the young man's flesh. He thinks perhaps she may have reached up on the way to the restaurant and plucked down one of the icicles hanging from the eaves and lunged it into his stomach under the cover of the table-cloth. He looks down with the shock of the pain and is surprised not to see blood upon his napkin mixing with rivulets of crystal icy water.

"Monica," he says, boyish perplexity wrinkling his forehead, "if this is so, if this is the way you feel, what have you been doing in my arms for the past six months?"

She takes her napkin from her lap and throws it upon the table-cloth.

He sees then that he has spoken out of turn, that he has spoken something which should have remained unsaid between them. But he determines to perceive it as an advantage, an advantage to be now pressed home.

He leans towards her, across the table, over the candle

and the condiments and the dusty plastic flowers and proceeds to tell her how she looks and how she feels in the act of love.

He uses the harshest of language, neither lowering his voice nor raising it, but speaking steadily and insistently so that the conversation of the two women at the next table peters away beneath its shocking perseverance and they fall silent, pretending to fidget with the carrier bags at their feet in order to draw a little nearer.

The longer he speaks, the cruder become his words and his phrases and the colder his voice.

"I have had you, Monica," he finishes, his eyes slanting with insinuation, "whimpering like an animal in my arms. Do not tell me you do not love me, Monica."

And yet he cannot touch her. An elusiveness in her, an evasion, defuses his anger, divesting his speech of its obscenity.

"Yes," she says. "Most probably I love you."

But her voice is cool and detached, as though she describes some innocuous failing in herself, some folly, some weakness, say for chocolates or cream cakes, to which she has become resigned.

"Then why, Monica, why?" he asks, banging the side of his hand down hard upon the table and turning heads across the room.

"I don't know," she says, shrugging her shoulders, drawing a fork across the table-cloth. "I don't know. Probably because it's not enough."

And now he is helpless in the face of her abstraction, helpless before her wandering eyes, before the opacity of her words. And so he tries a last blind thrust into the obfuscation which threatens to overwhelm him.

"He does not love you, Monica," he says boldly, unwisely. "He has affairs all the time. You know that. Almost since you were married."

"Yes, he has had affairs," she says. "But that does not mean he does not love me."

Her voice is very quiet and very deliberate and would serve as a warning were he not deaf to the sound of all but his own defeat.

And so he does not hear and goes on, blustering.

"He'll just go on having affairs. And then one day he'll

leave you for some student, probably"—his voice hardens with scorn—"and you'll wake up one morning middle-aged and alone."

"Probably not," she says, simply and quietly.

"How can you be so naïve, Monica?"

She looks at him, this child whom she loved but whom she knows now she never wanted to live with.

"Fidelity," she says with an old woman's smile, "is not everything in marriage."

"That's obscene."

And it is. For him it is. The real obscenity, the one that makes those he threw at her seem limp and inoffensive and really quite laughable. But her voice cuts back at him, sharp and quick.

"No! You don't understand. You can't understand. Having a husband who is faithful is like having a husband who is rich. It would be nice but you can manage without it."

The smile has returned. The voice is gentle. But he will not be placated. He feels the icicle lodged in his belly.

"And how do you *manage*, Monica?" he asks, suggestion curling his lips. "Do you *manage* with people like me keeping your spirits up? People like me, Monica, who thought they mattered to you and find out they were only helping you *manage?*"

He rains his bitterness down upon her bent head, but she appears impervious to the storm, merely follows the line of her finger trailing slowly and calmly up and down the stem of the ugly little vase.

"I see it all now, Monica," he says. "How could I have been so stupid."

He laughs gaily, speaking over-loudly like a man a little possessed. He slops wine messily into his glass from the large carafe he insisted upon ordering.

"I've been used, haven't I, Monica? You used me as he used his lovers. All of us, them and me, keeping your tawdry little marriage together. What is it we gave you, Monica, him and you? It's life blood, isn't it, Monica? That's what we gave you. You're a couple of vampires sucking the life blood from your lovers to pump back into your dead little marriage."

She rises sharply, scraping her chair back noisily and reaching for her handbag, but he is too quick for her.

He is up too and across the table, grabbing her hand and

pushing it down hard against the cloth, making the skin around her plain thin wedding ring white and bloodless with the pressure.

"I see it all, Monica," he repeats, his eyes boring into hers. "I thought I was something special but I was just part of a system. Can you believe it? There I was worrying seriously about the morality of breaking up your marriage when all the time I was just helping to keep it together."

He releases her hand and lowers himself slowly to his seat where he picks up his glass, his eyes fixed on his fingers around the stem.

"You fall in love with someone who is married and you think it's your story, hers and yours, you think it's your plot and your narrative and you think you're in charge. But then suddenly there's a twist in the plot and you find out that it was never your story at all. That it was someone else's story, her story and *his* story, their story together, the story that started long before you arrived on the scene, the story that will finish long after you've gone, the story in which you were just a chapter.

"It's funny, Monica," he says, raising his eyes to her as she stands buttoning her coat and winding her scarf around her neck, "I thought I was the hero, the leading man, but I wasn't, was I? I was just a character, a character like all the rest, not even a lesser character, but one of those minor characters who appear once or twice to nudge the plot along, one of those characters so unimportant they don't even warrant a name.

"What am I to you, Monica?" he asks, a bitter smile beginning to draw back the corners of his mouth.

"I'm a spear-carrier, aren't I? A bit-part player. A walk-on part."

And then as he speaks he notices the waiter, the waiter whom he thinks he recognises, who he thinks waved them off merrily that first night when they lost track of time and talked and talked through till the early hours, but who hovers now bemused and uncertain at the side of their table, a steaming plate of pasta in each hand.

Looking at him, the seated man smiles and shakes his head and leans back in his chair and swings his eyes, narrow with dislike, to the woman to extend a gallant arm to her, across the table, across the condiments and the carafe and the candle and across the ugly little vase.

"Dinner is served, Monica," he says, his voice stabbing the air between them. "Dinner is served."

Yes, he called her "Monica" and I too shall call her "Monica." It will be a special joke between us, he and I who do not know each other and never shall but who served in the same supporting cast.

Yes, I shall call her "Monica" in my book, which I shall begin when I have slept, when I have regained my strength. For I am very tired now and they have told me to sleep.

They said, "Sleep now. No more reading," and other things like "Don't worry" and "It happens." And once when they thought I was not listening they said, "There's always one. It's worse for them. The older ones. They're always more likely to overdo it."

I was reading, you see, that scene again, when there was a sound from the hall, an odd sound, a sort of pushing and scraping.

When I went out to see what was happening, I found the big black front-door key trembling in its lock.

As I knelt down before it on the old cold brown lino, it suddenly fell with a clatter at my feet.

"Everything is all right, Rose," came a voice, mumbling through the keyhole.

"I am here, Rose," it said softly against the brass.

"Nothing will happen to you, Rose. Not while I'm here, Rose."

"Thank you, Luis," I said.

"I understand it all now, Luis."

"I'm glad, Rose."

"It wasn't my story, Luis."

"If you say so, Rose."

"I was just a chapter, Luis."

"You may be right, Rose."

"Just a minor character, Luis."

"I see, Rose."

"I love him, Luis."

"I'm so sorry, Rose."

"I hope I didn't compromise you."

"No, not at all. For some obscure reason you kept calling me 'Luis.'"

He speaks the name as if he chips away at it, as if he chisels it on stone. It is cold in his mouth and awkward, and to cover his embarrassment at its use, he smiles his old jovial, jesterish smile.

"You don't say it like that. You make it sound like a tweed. It's not pronounced like the island or the shop. It's softer, more romantic, with a lot more "oooh" in it, as in Looooois."

I am smiling too, but smiling falsely, for the smile covers a sharp stab of irritation that thrusts through the camouflage of exaggerated politeness.

"So who is this Loooois anyway?"

"It's a long story."

You see, sadly, in spite of everything, his novel lied. It lied in spite of all that it told me. It lied in the way all novels lie when they give in to the temptation to round things off neatly, and in this I must say that David was right. Not that I don't understand the need for the blazing eyes and the harsh words of great moment and the white-knuckled hands clamped in forced and angry farewell upon the table. I do. I do. I understand. Today, believing there are no happy endings, we do the best we can with what we have. We dignify the sad ones that leave us unsatisfied and still wanting with a splendid last scene, a scene in which The End hangs suspended, trembling in the air above our heads, ready to crash down with a wonderful irrevocable whoosh at the end of the conversation, when we may allow the couple to part, with sadness certainly, but with the comfortable feeling at least that everything which should have been has indeed been spoken.

The problem being, of course, that life, the famous Life, isn't like that.

I know that, for here we are, Paul, and I, in what must pass for our parting scene, talking in low and reasoned tones of trivialities and inconsequences.

"Congratulations on your result. A good two-one."

"How did they mark me?"

"On your year's work. And of course on your novel."

"Oh yes, of course. I forgot. My novel."

Half of the exams were over, you see, by the time they found me. Jennifer went with them to the flat when I failed to turn up for the first one, but of course they found no one. Paul might have told them where I was, but he was away researching for his programme on Conrad.

By the time he returned I had smoked all the dope and lost ten pounds through not eating. I had also, by virtue of missing meals and scarcely sleeping, managed to read the novel thirty-seven times. I know that because I used to calculate it instead of counting sheep as I was about to drop off to sleep as once, when I was younger, I calculated the number of men I had been to bed with.

They had apparently been attempting to gain an entry for some time when Paul finally poked the key through the keyhole. They rang the bell continually until he remembered it didn't work and then hammered on the door. When I was finally persuaded to let them in, they took me to the university sanatorium where they put me to bed with explicit instructions to sleep.

Taking them at their word, I slept through the rest of the exams, waking occasionally to a world of whiteness, to eat and then sleep again. Several times, half waking, I opened my eyes to see a figure seated on the low chair beside the iron-railed bed pointing his puritanical little beard at me.

The last time it happened I said, "I'm glad you're here. I've been wanting to talk to you."

I said, "I understand now. The secret you held simmering inside. It was Margaret made me see it. Children. Our master-stroke. The way we overwhelm you. The way we win from the womb. And you saw it. And you tried to tell them. The awful possibility. That men may be just a means to an end.

"Priest and prophet . . ." I whispered drowsily, "keeper of the twisted key. . ."

Which is when he leaned forward and hissed at me, his head almost on my pillow.

"What about the dope, Rose?" he said.

"Oh, David," I said, "it's you."

"You didn't tell them who gave you the dope, Rose, did you?" he said insistently, pushing his face close to mine.

"What dope, David?" I asked sleepily.

"That's good, Rose," he said soothingly, leaning back. "That's good. I have your novel here. I think it's interesting. Lots of good points. I thought you'd like to talk about it."

"Some other time I think, David," I said, my eyes closing again. "I have to sleep now."

• • •

To this day I don't know if it happened.

Later I tried to make discreet enquiries of Jennifer.

"Did you come before," I said idly, "with David?"

"With David? How could we? Visitors were forbidden."

"It's nothing," I said. "I must have dreamt it."

Jennifer arrived bearing an exquisite bunch of perfectly budding pink roses and a basket of obscure and expensive fruit which she had dressed herself.

She screamed with horror when she saw the sanatorium's regulation canvas shift.

"You *can't* wear that thing," she said firmly, moving towards the door. "You look like Ophelia in the mad scene."

Half an hour later she was back with a beautiful long nightgown of bright white starched cotton.

"Jennifer..." I said in panic, looking at the price tag which dangled from the ruffled, high-buttoned neck.

"Forget it," she said brusquely. "A present. To cheer you up."

I won't hear a word against Jennifer.

Jo sent a bouquet, too, which I thought was particularly decent not only because she was busy pounding the pavements in the election but also because her house was burgled the day after they took me away.

The thieves, faced with a twenty-year-old radio, an old black-and-white TV and a Dansette record player, took the Russian flag and the Che Guevara poster, probably, I feel, out of pique.

They let me out on the day of the election, in the first place because I insisted I had to vote, and in the second because Helen assured them she would look after me.

And so it was that I was able to go to the polling station to put an "X" against Martin's name, thus shakily adding my signature to the metaphorical International Declaration on Masculine Rights which states that cheating on his wife should not disbar a man from public office.

And so it was also that Helen and I were able to watch Jo standing at the mayor's elbow, her huge rosette overshadowed by a wide foolish grin quite out of place upon her fine intelligent face, a slim, surprisingly girlish wrist

raised in the air to acknowledge the cheers of her sup-
porters. And all this knowing she had lost.

"What sort of woman would put herself through that?"
Helen said, her whisky glass raised to her lips before the
television, her arm clutched around her knees beneath the
white towelling dressing gown.

We saw Martin raise a hand in the air, too, but in his
case in victory, in delight even, having, in these testing
political times, increased his majority.

Beside him Margaret waved, too, waved and smiled, but
rather coolly I thought, a very smart Margaret in the expensive jacket and black dress, hair bristling punkily on
top of her head.

Yes, Margaret waved too and so did their daughter,
whom they brought with them onto the dais, Janet, fourteen and growing up fast, blond and very pretty in jeans
and a T-shirt with a pink fluorescent badge the size of a
saucer pinned to her chest and on it the words, "Behind
every successful man is an exhausted woman."

Maybe it was the badge that did it. Certainly Helen got
very drunk on election night.

It was pretty much all over, including the shouting, when
she snapped down the sound and demanded, "Do you know
how many days I've had off sick in the last six years?"

"No, I don't know. How many?"

"Go on. Guess."

When we got there eventually it was two. She waved the
fingers around in the air above her head like the horns of a
cuckold.

"No wonder he loves me," she said gloomily.

Later she asked, pacing up and down before the newly
restored picture window, "Do I really want to be married to
this man as well as work for him?"

"Probably not," I said.

"Damn right not," she answered, banging her glass down
hard upon the sideboard with the air of one who has made
a decision.

"Sandra knows he won't leave her and she's happy," she

said, lifting the whisky bottle and re-filling the glass. "And guess what? I know he won't leave her and I've suddenly realised that I think I'm happy as well."

"What about him?"

"Him," she said, smiling through the first slug of her drink. "Ah yes, him. Him will just have to fend for himself."

The next morning she got Andy off to school and then called work, telling them briskly that she would not be in.

The switchboard operator had the misfortune to ask if she would like to leave any messages or instructions, if she would like to speak to someone, perhaps to Ray. She replied sweetly and icily that she would not, that she had no desire to speak to anyone, unless perhaps it be to her pillow with whom she could discuss the peculiarly excruciating nature of her hangover.

The next day she hummed as she made Andy's breakfast, parping the horn in a particularly jaunty fashion as she drove off to work.

There apparently she strode straight into Ray's office, turfing out without ceremony an unwise employee asking for a raise before coffee time.

Sitting down on the newly vacated seat, she crossed her legs firmly and told Ray she would be taking two months' holiday, effective from the following day.

She cited, by way of explanation, her calculation which had discovered, to her surprise, that she had only had two days off sick in the past six years.

She reminded him, in addition, of the taxing time she had had over the past year. The separation had been... painful. As well as everything else. She looked at him steadfastly as he stood above her leaning his knuckles on the desk so that he dropped his eyes, apparently in some shame.

Anyway, she said briskly, now she was very tired. She needed a complete break. And she needed time also to see solicitors about the divorce. To put the house up for sale. She was sick of trying to fit it all in around work. Then she was going to take a holiday. With Rose. She thought somewhere exotic. Where she could get a complete rest. Thailand, say, or Bali. Perhaps even the Philippines. "Rose has been there before," she said.

Michael would take Andy for a few weeks while she was away. He'd like that. And of course Kathy adored children. Michael could also show people around the house. They thought it should sell quickly. It had always been, after all, a highly desirable development. So near the town centre and yet with its green. "So terribly villagey," she said.

She crossed her hands upon her raised knee, assuming a pose of utterly reasonable inflexibility. She said she realised she was asking for a long break and at such short notice. She could see that it might cause difficulties. But she knew for her own state of health she had to have it. So she had no choice, she said. If necessary she would resign.

She said all this smiling at him in a friendly fashion.

Opposite her Ray rolled gently down to earth on the balls of his soft-shod feet, stopped chewing and for once was still, saying, "Yes ma'am," or to be more precise, "Of course, Helen," and "Anything you say, Helen," and "Come home rested, Helen."

And thrown into a funk as blue as his beloved Rolls-Royce at her positively cavalier use of the word "resign," he insisted that the holiday, "Rose's, too," should be written off as a business expense to reward her for all her hard work in the past. He then went on to press upon her, with some warmth, first a substantial pay rise and then a considerably more luxurious company car.

"Don't leave me, Helen," he finished pleadingly.

Jennifer got a first, which surprised no one, and was married two weeks after graduation.

Helen was at the wedding and so was I, but Jo was away in Greece. With Marcus.

"He's insisting on paying," she said, "so really I thought I might as well say yes. Says it's his way of apologising. Really he's not that bad, Marcus, and I need a couple of weeks lying on a beach doing nothing. God, I'm so tired. Must have walked twenty miles a day canvassing. And I need some time to think. They want me to stand again. I'm thinking of selling the house. Moving back down there. We need to build the party up again. Heal the splits. We've let the seat slip away from us. But he only scraped in. You saw the result. A couple of hundred votes. It was a fluke. We'll win it back next time. You'll see."

Jennifer asked me to fill out a wedding form for her local paper.

"After all, Rose, you're the writer," she laughed.

And so I did, duly recording that Jennifer was married in the fifteenth-century church in the border village where she was brought up and wore an exquisite ankle-length off-the-shoulder dress of cream silk, deeply sashed at the waist, with her hair in an upswept style beneath a large picture hat, and carried a small bouquet of rare orchids, and was attended by her six-year-old niece, Pandora, who wore the same style of dress, with a posy in her hands and tiny picture hat too upon her head.

I did not forget to state, either, that a reception was held afterwards on the lawn at the bride's home, that the flowers in the church and in the marquee were done by the bride's aunt (well-known locally for her floral demonstrations) and that the cake was made by her sister, a professional *cordon bleu* caterer in London, and that the reception included friends from university, from where the bride recently graduated and where she met her husband, a poet, who was writer in residence there.

Oh yes, and naturally I concluded by informing readers that the bride left for her brief honeymoon in Paris in an olive green "combat-style" trouser suit off-set with a toning crêpe de Chine blouse.

I still feel I should have stepped forward in that ghastly theatrical moment when I was asked, along with the rest, if I could show any just cause why David and Jennifer should not be joined together in holy matrimony.

Stepped forward? Why? For whom? For Francie? Perhaps. But to say what?
"Some just cause?"
"No, not exactly, but..."

At the reception we drank our champagne and ate our smoked salmon sandwiches and our strawberries and cream and indulged ourselves in pretentious conversations about how it took a wedding to remind us of the importance of ritual in non-religious societies and of how much poorer the language would be for the loss of Biblical imagery.

It was a hot, overblown day, and Jennifer and David and Helen and I had separated ourselves from the rest of the guests, sitting on a low rockery wall beneath a shady beech tree.

Jennifer leaned back in her cream silk and surveyed a beautifully shaved sunbed-tanned leg and a perfectly polished toe-nail peeping through an expensive open-toed shoe.

Next to her, David, in shirt sleeves, looking particularly Lawrentian with the waistcoat of his morning suit unbuttoned to reveal his braces, smoked a joint with ostentatious ease.

Helen, eyes closed, stretched out upon the lawn, a dried-up piece of grass at her lips.

"I hate weddings," I said, a little drunk from too much champagne. "To do this thing. In public. Not even in the privacy of your own home. But before people. It's absurd. Indecent. Positively tribal."

"What's indecent, Rose?" said Jennifer, snuggling closer to David's white-shirted chest. "You mean the part about obeying?"

"Obeying? No. There's nothing wrong with obeying. I'd obey if I could find one worth obeying. It would be a positive relief. No, I mean the 'forsaking all others' bit. That's the nitty gritty, isn't it? I mean never mind all this stuff about loving and comforting. Forget the cherishing. I mean he'll still manage to cherish you in his own way even when he's got another bit going on the side. No. It's the 'forsaking all others' that's the clincher. The 'honour her'—that's the bit that really counts."

There was silence for a moment. Outside the patch of cool dark shade the violent blue sky and the merciless sun seemed to bear down on the brittle brown dried-up garden.

Then Helen spoke, her eyes still closed, the grass teasing her lips.

"I'm not sure fidelity's that important," she said. "But then. Look at me. I'm still friends with the woman who screwed my husband."

"My God, you know." I shot forward off the wall, spilling my drink.

"Of course I know. I saw you."

"My God. In the Wendy house."

"I had high hopes of you, Rose," she said, laughing. "But you let me down badly. I thought with a bit of luck he might leave me for you. He was quite besotted, you know. But unfortunately you turned out to be smarter than I thought and wouldn't have anything more to do with him. Actually I felt quite offended on his behalf.

"Really," she said, "I don't know why I'm still friends with you. You treated my husband quite abominably."

"Ah yes, my novel."

"I've been wanting to see you. To tell you. I read it. I was very impressed. When I last spoke to you about it you were having some problem with the ending, I remember..."

He didn't come to see me, you see. Not at the sanatorium. Not at Helen's. He didn't come to see me and he didn't call, and by the time I finally came home I no longer expected it.

I had stopped planning in my head, as I did in the sanatorium, the perfect parting. Myself, the wronged Victorian heroine, pale and agitated but pretty as a picture in Jennifer's nightie in the low chair. And him perched upon the window-sill, dangling legs making an awkward geometric figure against the white wall, unable to meet my eyes, looking away in shame as he prized the slats of the blind apart with embarrassed fingers.

I had stopped planning how I would scorch him with my eyes and with what I had to say, each word astute and appropriate and impeccably in place, and how I would see him leave, without a word, slinking out through the door, a changed and chastened man.

I had stopped planning all this, which is just as well, for here he is before me now, sipping his coffee with no show of concern or disquiet, biting into his brownie and telling me about Monica.

"She's been told she has to rest. With being an older mother, you know. So I've been looking after the bookshop for her several days a week. Which has made life absolutely frantic for me, of course, because we've actually started filming the Conrad programme. And believe it or not they're already talking about another. They're suggesting something similar on Lawrence. Although of course I've tried to dissuade them. I'm of your opinion. Enough is enough, for a while at least, on Lawrence, I feel."

He was here, serving a customer, ringing up the money and putting the books into a bag, when I came in to buy travel guides for our holiday.

He was absurdly jocular and enthusiastic, calling to Francie, "Look after the shop for a minute, will you? This is Rose. One of my ex-students. I want to take her downstairs for a coffee."

She turned her head and looked at me, a long, flat, empty stare, and then nodded at him, without speaking, turning back to the bookshelves.

And so here he is, selfish to the last, trying to deny me my ending, wanting me to exchange pleasantries and niceties, wanting me to mend and make do, wanting me to compromise and be civil and count as a conclusion this accidental, ambiguous, thoroughly feeble little finale.

But he won't get away with it. I won't give in. I've got one last card to play. It's a special card. An unexpected card. The joker in the pack which here I take out and lay face up before us on the table.

"I've started a new novel now, Paul. It's about adultery."

He was making snide little comments about the shortcomings of his producer when I broke in on him, stopping him mid-stream. Now he takes a cigarette slowly from a packet and reaches to the food bar for an ashtray, which he slides with deliberation upon the table.

"It's going very well," I say. "Positively racing ahead, in fact."

Before me he lights up the cigarette, staring intently at the flame. He shakes the match out and tosses it lightly into the ashtray. When finally he speaks, the light, polite and chatty voice is quite gone. Instead it is abrupt and full of suppressed anger and heavy with resignation.

"I'm in it, of course?"

"No. Not at all. There is someone a bit like you. But I've made him more charming and cleverer and much better-looking, oh yes, and better in bed. So don't worry. No one will recognise you."

He takes in a long thin breath of the cigarette and lets it out in a smoke ring that is weak and thin and unsuccessful and disintegrates immediately above his head.

"I never know when you're joking, Rose," he says coldly.

"I'm always joking," I say, smiling. "Only all my jokes are serious."

"Fair game," I say, "writers' integrity and all that."

"Here's to Trigorin," I say, raising the last of my freshly filtered coffee as a toast in the air.

"Here's to Trigorin."

20

T H E Y don't gather round to watch you if you weep on trains in England. They don't put delicacies in your lap. No, they fix their eyes upon their papers, or shake the pages out ostentatiously and hrrumph and clear their throats, saying with all of these things, "Come, come. Enough of this. Dry your eyes now and in return I will pretend I never saw you crying."

We hired a car one day, Helen and I, and drove out to the hacienda only to find it silent and shuttered. The back door, though, had been forced and stood open, groaning a little in the gathering wind, as if in shame at the nature of the crime and the evidence of the violation, the rusting tin cans and the empty cardboard boxes, and the animal droppings, heaped by some wicked chance in a small sacramental pile in the very spot where once I cried out among the snowy pillowcases upon the dark wood bed.

And then outside the bedroom, walking away down the wood-panelled corridor, a naked toe poking through my sandal touched something light and cold and skittered it tinkling along the stones. It caught in the shaft of light from the door at the end, a spent cartridge from a rifle.

I woke him up one night as he slept against the wall, whispering in his ear and touching him lightly on the shoulder. "Wake up, Luis, wake up. I want to go swimming."

He woke slowly, rubbing his hand across his eyes misty with sleep.

"I want to go swimming, Luis," I said again, and he got to his feet, dropping the rifle with a clatter upon the flags.

He went to the door and whistled softly, but I stopped him, calling quietly into the darkness.

"No guards, Luis. Just you and me."

In the jeep, sitting beside him, I rested his rifle across my knees, exploring the feel of the trigger against my finger.

I called "Come, Luis" as I ran into the water, cracking its crystal stillness, but he only shook his head and smiled and lay back on the sand smoking, his head upon the crook of his arm.

The sand was as silky white as untanned skin in the moonlight as I sat down beside him in a bright sarong, still wet from the swim. The sea was as dark and still and unfathomable as his eyes, as above us a soft breeze stirred and rustled in the tops of the coconut trees as if waiting like me for him to speak.

"There have been others here before you, Rose," he said eventually, croaking a little as he drew in a deep breath from the joint.

"There will be others after you have gone."

Walking around we found a solitary old woman washing clothes at the waterfall, thrashing them upon a stone as she raised her face to us, cackling and smiling through black and broken teeth.

I tried to ask her what had happened at the hacienda, but she only smiled and cackled some more. I tried again at a bar in the nearby town, but there the owner would only shrug his shoulders and grimace and shake his head before bringing us more beer, leaving us to drive away unsatisfied.

We went to the beach then and lay on the empty crescent of sand, becoming hotter and more lazy and more unwilling to leave as the afternoon went on, so that it was late when we arrived back at the hotel to find the telegram waiting.

I was lying on the bed, stretched out and sleepy, when the door opened very slowly and she came in, the white piece of paper in her hand.

I laughed and would have said, "What's the news from the boardroom," for I knew when the receptionist told us about the wire that it must be from Ray, wooing Helen home. But then I saw the way she moved across the room and the words died in my throat.

For she moved slowly and awkwardly in the gloom, her body dark from the sun and angular in her shorts and tiny top so that for a brief moment she reminded me of Francie.

Her face was dark too and very blank, and she sat upon the bed thoughtfully and carefully, as if the business of living had been temporarily erased from her mind and because of this she had forgotten even the simple act of sitting.

As she sat she crumpled the white piece of paper behind her back, pushing it away in irritation with short, sharp impotent jabs, but it rolled back down the coverlet until I pulled it gently away from her hands and read it.

It said, "Sandra in hospital. Cancer. Come home. Please. Ray."

I stared at the words, and at Helen's name, and the name of the hotel, as if trying to piece them all together in a different way, to make a different message, one that might not mean what it said or might be discovered, after all, to belong to someone else. I was still staring when I heard the springs squeak and felt the bed give.

When I looked up she was leaning her head against the white wall, below a wooden crucifix, between the dark wardrobe and the window.

Then slowly but with deliberation she began to strike her head against the wall, with each movement spitting out a sharp, vicious "shit."

For a moment I watched her, hypnotised by the cathartic rhythm of the movement, and then I jumped up and pulled her roughly from the wall and held her for a moment, the white-wash from her forehead weeping on my shoulder, till her whole body suddenly went rigid in my arms, rising up like a column and funnelling up into the air a great rush of shame and disgust and self-dislike which washed back down over both of us.

"Oh no, oh no, oh no, oh no," she cried.

No, they don't put delicacies in your lap if you weep on trains in England. They draw themselves up and fold themselves in and pull down the blinds of their eyes, fearing you will turn and tell them for whom it is you are crying.

She released herself from my arms, excusing herself with a small apologetic bow of her head and a sad smile that thinned and lengthened and withdrew into a taut, unapproachable line. Which is how it stayed while she dealt with the formalities, the re-arranged flights, the cancelled hotels, the phone call to Ray. Which is how it stayed until a moment ago, when she turned her head to the dull East Coast countryside unravelling northwards past the carriage window, and with one long, blank unhappy stare put her head back upon the seat and closed her eyes, whereupon the lips gently began to quiver, finally stretching themselves in one long contortion of despair as she very quietly, very discreetly, and without embarrassment, began to cry.

They'll measure Sandra and match her up and give her one of those wonderful garments that makes it look as though nothing has happened. And if the gold jewellery has nowhere to trickle to, never mind. It was always her smile that drew people to Sandra.

They say Sandra will be all right, you see. They say they caught it in time. They say the operation was a hundred per cent successful and barring any recurrence, anything unforeseen...

But despite all this, Helen is frightened. The thin tight line of her lips, which drew in her fear and held it, has snapped so that now it escapes, slipping out beneath the closed eyes in clumsy crystal drops. She fears this thing, this cancer, and because of this her fear grows within her like a cancer itself, chewing away at her slowly and insidiously with its horrible insinuation.

She fears, you see, she knows a truth about this thing called "cancer," a simple truth she thinks is learnt by women living every day, a simple truth she thinks escapes those searching for it in the laboratory.

She thinks she knows how cancer begins for such as Sandra. She thinks it begins with a gently gnawing unhappiness and grows with grief, working its way down through from the heart to the body, to leave the darkly innocent shadow upon the X-rays.

She fears that this thing, this "cancer," comes of sadness and disappointment, of betrayal and loss of love. She is superstitious, with an old fear, a woman's fear, a fear that tells her to believe an old wives' tale which says that sickness is a seed caught up upon the wind, whirling about the world and seeking heavy hearts to nestle in, seeking loneliness and disappointment and loss of self-esteem to feed itself upon.

And now she fears her guilt. She fears her crime. But most of all she fears the punishment. She fears the small and darkened room, the white-sleeved arm that leads her in and switches on the light, and clamps between it and herself, with a forceful and determined clash, the photograph, the proof, her own face shining back, in charming cameo between the blurred and whitened bones.

And, as for me, I do not like that old joke now, that joke told by men in too-tight dinner jackets to too much smokey laughter. And I shall not tell my own joke now, that tale I tell about my Romeo to make my women laugh.

If you want a joke, I'll tell you a joke. I'll give you something to laugh at, something droll, a little whimsicality, a jest, a jape, a small conceit.

I'll give you Sandra, Sandra lovely Sandra, golden glowing Amazon, captured queen, raising herself naked from the bed, lowering her fine long-columned legs to the floor to stand, the soft roundness of her belly narrowing to the burnt gold bush of her hair, her head thrown back, tousled and streaked and catching the light above the smooth dampness of her face, walking towards you with that smile, that smile wide and warm and welcoming, above that one full, fine and softly swaying breast.

I said to him in parting, picking up my bag, "Remember me to Monica."

It was a cheap, unpleasant throw-away remark.

He said, "Ah yes, Monica," his voice still cold and unfriendly.

"As a matter of fact," he said, "Monica mentioned you this morning."

"Oh really. How cosy. Over breakfast, was it? What did she say?"

"She was asking about you. I explained that you'd been ill during the exams. She said she was sorry. She said she'd been thinking of you. That was all. She said she'd been thinking of you."

And then he said to me, he said, because we still at heart are animals and turn and snap and snarl at those we think have turned and snapped and snarled at us, "This novel. I suppose it's full of female pain?"

His voice was heavy and cold and sarcastic, but flat too with a sense of its own failure, for he had wanted the words to come out light and unconcerned, a witty parting shot between us.

And looking at him, I was lost for words. I could think of no way of answering him, no way of dealing with the sickness at what he had said. As I stared at him I felt the distance, drawing us back and back until, looking down, I saw the great gulf fixed between us, man and woman, and saw the hopelessness of its width and its depth and the waste of the broken dreams that could not span it lying fallen and scattered on its stony bed.

And I was astonished, not that such as he and I should have had an affair, only that we should be expected to live on the same planet together.

And, unable to think of anything to say that could be said quickly and conveniently across the coffee table, and being also a little frightened at what I had seen, I pushed my chair in neatly towards him and placed carefully the strap of my bag over my shoulder and smiled, by way of conciliation.

"Yes," I said. "I suppose it's full of female pain."